Rivers of Grace

Rivers of Grace

Raising Children by the Spirit
Rather than the Law

Mark and Patti Virkler

Sovereign World

Sovereign World Ltd
PO Box 777
Tonbridge

Kent TN11 0ZS
England

ISBN 1 85240 352 7

Cover design by CCD, www.ccdgroup.co.uk
Typeset by CRB Associates, Reepham, Norfolk
Printed in the United States of America

Dedication

To Charity and Joshua
With much love.

Your lives are a tribute to the glory of God's grace.
We are so proud of you!

Contents

Author's note

Mark and Patti have been writing books together for nearly thirty years. Sometimes Mark is the main author and researcher, and sometimes Patti is. Whichever of them does the actual writing, they are both wholly involved in each project, discussing, analyzing, adjusting, confirming, correcting and editing. They therefore consider all of their books as joint ventures, and list themselves both as authors.

Introduction

I was never really crazy about kids. I was the youngest child in my family, and never spent much time around younger children. I did some babysitting in my teen years, but that was only to earn spending money, not because of the pleasure I received from the job. Babies always seemed so fragile. And between the dribble and the diapers, they were messy and icky. Toddlers were just miniature noise machines with only one setting – loud and fast. And they knew only two words: "NO!" and "MINE!"

I majored in elementary education in college. I did my student teaching in first and third grades, and frankly, I wasn't very good at it. I was terribly self-conscious and nervous around the children. And teenagers simply terrified me. From what I observed, they were nothing but a bad attitude wrapped in weird clothes.

Then, two days before my twenty-fifth birthday, our daughter Charity was born. You have never seen such a beautiful little girl! Wavy brown hair, huge brown eyes, deep dimples, and a smile that would melt your heart. Two years later, she was joined by her brother Joshua, the most beautiful little boy ever born. Curly blond hair, huge blue eyes, and the sweetest disposition you can imagine. These babies were bright and healthy and happy and a constant joy to my heart. And, did I mention how beautiful they were? Every minute with them was pure pleasure. Caring for their needs was an absolute delight. I found that even the dribbles and diapers were just opportunities to coax a precious giggle out of their loving little hearts.

All my life I have heard about the "terrible twos and threes." Well, somehow we missed those years. We had the terrific twos and tremendous threes! Toddlers are so much fun! Everything is new and exciting and interesting. Mom and Dad are brilliant fountains of all wisdom and knowledge, strong towers of refuge who can do no wrong. Oh, I absolutely loved those years!

The Lord called us to teach our children at home when Charity was just three years old. At that time, homeschooling was basically unknown. It was not unusual for Social Services to remove your children from your home for truancy and arrest you for child neglect if you were homeschooling. But God put it in our hearts that this was His will and purpose for us, and I am so glad He did. Homeschooling our two children has been the single most satisfying thing I have ever done.

Those elementary years were so fulfilling. Children are created to learn, and they absolutely love to do so, if we don't crush that desire through competition, insensitivity, or boredom. Besides the "book learning," every Wednesday was family day. We went to parks, museums, Niagara Falls, Chuck E. Cheese, libraries and amusement parks. We explored the creek, the woods, the beach, and our own backyard. We toured power plants, factories, bakeries, and waste treatment facilities. We went roller-skating, bowling, sledding, bike riding, ice-skating, and hiking. And then we did it all again!

Gradually time passed and we approached the dreaded teen years. I had been taught that rebellion was a natural part of growing up, and that repudiating your parents and their values was a normal, expected, and even necessary part of the maturing process. I personally rejected those beliefs as lies from the pit soon after my children were born. To imagine that my precious children would one day turn against me, to believe that I had to *expect* that, was totally unacceptable to me. Proverbs 10:22 (KJV) declares, *"The blessing of the Lord, it maketh rich, and he addeth no sorrow with it."* I claimed that promise for my life. I knew that my children were a blessing from the Lord that had greatly enriched me, and I believed that they would add no sorrow to my life, but only joy. Praise God, He has been faithful to that promise!

As our children grew and matured, we continued to spend

lots of time together. I taught them at home all the way
through high school. (They never attended traditional
school.) We ate our meals together, played together, worked
together, and vacationed together. They became our best
friends. There has been no hint of rebellion or "normal" teen
attitude in their relationship with us. Not that they haven't
questioned and explored and examined our beliefs and standards. They have, and they still are. But it has been with respect
and honor, not rebellion or disrespect.

Now they are young adults. Charity traveled to eighteen
countries before her eighteenth birthday, sometimes with us
and often with various mission endeavors. She spent a year in
Tulsa in the Teen Mania Ministries internship program, and
now she is back home, completing her post-graduate studies
before God leads her into the next exciting adventure He has
planned for her. She loves to meditate on the Scriptures and
claims the Holy Spirit as her closest friend. She knows she will
one day influence the world, and is preparing for the day
when the Lord calls her to step forward into her destiny.

Joshua is our resident computer expert and government
watchdog/activist. He also lives at home, pursuing external
degree studies in those two main areas of his interest. He is
our diplomat, quietly listening and observing, hearing all
points of view, drawing others into more clearly communic-
ating their ideas, then laying out the overall picture that ties it
all together. Sometimes I look at these two young adults and
am moved to tears at the goodness and grace of God, that He
has allowed me the privilege of knowing and loving such
special people.

For the last few years, Mark has been urging me to write a
book about raising children. Seeing the different philosophies
and methods other parents use, Chari and Josh have added
their support to Mark's encouragement. I have resisted for two
major reasons.

First, my training is not in the area of family therapy, child
development or psychology. Isn't it presumptuous for me to
think I have anything to contribute to these disciplines when
there are so many more learned individuals writing and
teaching on these subjects? My second reason for hesitating
to write this book was my conviction that it is largely by the

grace of God that Charity and Joshua are who they are today. I have seen too many godly families suffer the pain of wayward children to believe that somehow we did anything to "deserve" to be spared that tragedy.

But lately the Lord has been showing me that, just as we can put up blockages that prevent the grace of God from flowing in our lives, there are also things we can do to clear the way for His grace. And that is an area in which I have been trained. Mark and I have devoted our lives to learning how to increase the flow of God's grace in the lives of believers and developing training materials to pass that knowledge on to others.

Let me clarify what I mean when I talk about the grace of God. The basic meaning of the Hebrew word for *grace* is "favor," while the New Testament Greek word connotes that it is a divine gratuity (perk, "freebie," bonus, benefit, extra). It is a free gift. It is forgiveness and deliverance. It is the divine influence upon the heart, and its reflection in the life.[1]

To me, grace is the essence of God's relationship with me. It is unmerited favor – God's goodwill toward me even though I don't deserve it. It is the mercy of God on sinful man. It is the power of God freely used for the benefit of frail mortals. It is God calling me to Himself before I even knew Him, and God calling me to holiness now that I am His child. It is God at work in me, giving me the desire and the ability to please Him. It is He Who began a good work in me, and He Who completes that work in me.

" 'Twas grace that taught my heart to fear, and grace my fears relieved." It was God's grace that showed me I needed salvation, and it was God's grace that provided me with salvation. It is grace that reveals dark areas that remain in my heart, and grace that drives the darkness out with the light of His presence. It is grace that gives me the desire and the strength to cling to the grace that gives me power over the enemy! It is all by grace, and it is amazing.

God has a vast reservoir of grace that He wants to pour into your life, your home, and your family. And He has provided lots of ways by which that grace can be channeled into your world. Unfortunately, these rivers of grace can become littered with the debris of our own sinful thoughts and actions, as well as the ungodly actions of our ancestors, creating dams that prevent His grace from flowing the way He desires.

My goal for this book is to help you clear away any obstructions that are preventing the grace of God from flowing freely in your family life, and help you establish great open channels by which His grace and mercy can pour in. That is my prayer for you. You may discover that what I have to say is very basic, and I would have to agree with you. Essentially, the concepts of this book could be reduced to the simple imperative, "Apply your Christianity to your family life!" I do hope, however, that what I have to say will spur you to new understandings and new ways of doing so.

During my years as a parent, I have read many, many books on raising children. I have especially been encouraged and instructed by the teachings of Kevin Leman, Gary Smalley, and James Dobson. These men have offered their years of education and experience to help young parents through the often confusing and always challenging process of raising godly children. After reading this book, you will still want to turn to them for advice on practical day-to-day matters of training and discipline. I would not presume to suggest that what I have to say in any way replaces or contradicts their wisdom.

What I want to offer are some spiritual principles that have not often been applied to family life. I hope I am able to stimulate you to new ways of looking at the dynamics of a family that lives in and reflects God's love every moment of every day. Of course, these principles will be most effective if you begin practicing them even before your children are born. But no matter how old your children are, and no matter what your relationship is with them today, if you will draw on the grace of God to change *you*, breaking down the barriers that have prevented His grace from flowing freely through you into your family, the river of the Spirit will sweep through your home bringing the righteousness, peace and joy of the kingdom of God into your world.

I am indebted to the teaching of many other leaders in the body of Christ for much of what I have to say in this book. Rather than try to reiterate all that has been said by others on each principle, I recommend to you the books listed in the

Bibliography. They will provide you with the detailed scriptural support and theological foundations you may need to move more confidently into any new areas.

Most of us grow and change most quickly and completely in the context of a group that shares the same goals. The accountability, support, and encouragement of fellow travelers on the way make the path easier and lots more fun. That is why I want to strongly encourage you to use this book with one or more friends.

Most of the rivers of grace we will talk about will require you to change your own behavior and develop new habits. This isn't easy, especially if you try to do it alone. Your first and greatest Helper, of course, is the Holy Spirit, Who wants to and is well able to make you into a pure channel through whom the grace of God flows in its fullness. But God has also placed His children in a body and made us part of a family. He wants us to be instruments of grace to one another as well, helping each other draw upon all the power of God that dwells within us. Appendix D offers ideas and suggestions for your group gatherings.

Note
1. Biblesoft's New Exhaustive Strong's Numbers and Concordance with Expanded Greek-Hebrew Dictionary. Copyright ©1994, Biblesoft and International Bible Translators, Inc.

Chapter 1

Start with a Clean Slate

Although Abraham eventually became known as "the Father of Faith," he had to grow in faith, just like we do. Twice when he entered new kingdoms while he was traveling to the Promised Land, he feared for his life. His wife Sarah was so gorgeous that every man that saw her wanted her for himself. Abraham was afraid that he would be attacked and killed by a foreign king wanting to add Sarah to his harem. So Abraham made a plan.

Both Sarah and Abraham had Terah as their father, although they each had a different mother. Therefore they were half-brother and sister before they were husband and wife. Abraham decided to take advantage of this technicality of their relationship to carry out a "minor" deception on the Pharaoh of Egypt and King Abimelech. He would tell them the truth about their relationship, but only part of the truth. "She is my sister," he said, and allowed her to be taken from him to become the wife of other men. So began the seed of deception that plagued Abraham's family for generations.

Abraham's son Isaac wasn't very creative in his deception. His wife Rebekah was also very, very beautiful, and he also feared for his life by those who would want her for themselves. So, since Abraham's little deception had worked so well (!), Isaac tried it for himself. "She is my sister," he told the Philistines, though she was actually only his second cousin. And the deception grew as the sin was passed to another generation.

Isaac grew old, as men tend to do, and was nearing death. He had two sons, twins, but not identical. Esau was the elder and thus had the birthright to the greater blessing. Jacob was the younger, and wanted the greater blessing. So he followed in the footsteps of his father and grandfather, and used deception to get his way. Dressing in his brother's best clothes and using the skin of a goat, he pretended to be Esau and thus received the blessing of the firstborn. And the sin was found in another generation.

Jacob went on to have twelve sons of his own, but he loved Joseph the best. His other sons were jealous of his love for their little brother and, when the opportunity presented itself, they got him out of their way. Using his best clothes and the blood of a goat, they deceived their father into believing that a wild animal had killed him. It was Jacob's son Judah who actually had the idea to sell Joseph as a slave and only pretend that he was dead. And the sin made its way through another generation.

Judah went on to marry and have three sons of his own. When the first was old enough, he married a woman named Tamar. But Judah's son was wicked, and God killed him before he could have any children. According to the custom of the time, Judah's second son was required to marry his brother's widow and give his firstborn son as his brother's heir. But this second son was also wicked and refused to give Tamar a child. So the Lord killed him, too.

Judah's third son was quite a bit younger than his brothers, so even though he would eventually be expected to marry Tamar and provide heirs for both of the deceased men, Tamar was sent home to wait until he grew up. Time passed, and the youngest boy matured. But after losing two of his sons who were married to Tamar, Judah was afraid that the third son would meet the same fate, so he didn't call Tamar back to marry him. Eventually, Tamar became aware of Judah's treachery and came up with a plan of her own. Changing her clothes to disguise herself as a prostitute, she deceived Judah about her identity and seduced him to sleep with her in exchange for a promised goat, and she became pregnant.

When Judah learned that she was pregnant by a man that was not his son, he was furious and demanded her death. At the last moment, she revealed the truth of her deception, and Judah accepted the consequences of his behavior. And the sin of deception played a major role in the lives of another generation.

"Like father, like son."
"The acorn doesn't fall far from the tree."
"He sure has his father's temper!"
"What a gossip – just like her mother!"

When you look in the mirror, are you beginning to see your parents? Do you find yourself struggling with the same weaknesses and frustrations that plagued their lives?

Does a tendency toward addiction "run in your family"? Is there a hereditary illness that torments you and your relatives?

Is there a certain besetting sin that hounds members of your family across generational lines, no matter how committed to the Lord the individual? Is there a "character flaw" that keeps showing its ugly face?

Do you think it is cute when your three-year-old sticks out his chin, looking just like his grandpa, his eyes cold with anger when things don't go his way?

Does it make you uneasy to see your seven-year-old's face falling into the same sullen lines of discontent that characterize your mother?

Have your brothers and sisters borne sons and daughters but not enjoyed them, because they were taken captive by ungodly music, peer pressure, alcohol, *Dungeons and Dragons*, drugs, violent video games, illicit sex, petty crime? Do you fear the day when your children are tempted by these enemies – fear it so much that you have bound your children in rules and laws and regulations that attempt to control not only their actions, but their minds and hearts as well?

Does your child suffer from unexplained pains and illnesses – fevers, rashes, tumors, sores that won't heal or keep recurring? Is she "accident-prone"?

Does success seem right within your grasp, only to slip away time and again?

Is there a cloud of darkness that follows you wherever you go, paralyzing you into confusion, depression or indecision?

At work, do others constantly get the credit, bonuses and promotions that you deserve for your ideas and innovations, while you remain stuck in your dead-end position?

Perhaps there is something other than mere bad luck at work in your life and family. Perhaps you are dealing with more than environmental influences and learned behaviors. Perhaps you are battling something deeper than genetics, and stronger than habits.

> *"I, the* Lord *your God, am a jealous God, punishing the children for the sin of the fathers* **to the third and fourth generation** *of those who hate me . . . "*   (Exodus 20:5)

> *"No one born of a forbidden marriage* [or 'a bastard' – KJV] *nor any of his descendants may enter the assembly of the* Lord, **even down to the tenth generation.***"*
>   (Deuteronomy 23:2)

> *"If you do not obey the* Lord *your God and do not carefully follow all his commands and decrees I am giving you today, all these curses will come upon you and overtake you . . .* **the fruit of your womb will be cursed** *. . . "*
>   (Deuteronomy 28:15,18)

> *"The* Lord *will afflict you with the boils of Egypt and with tumors, festering sores and the itch, from which you cannot be cured. The* Lord *will afflict you with madness, blindness and confusion of mind."*   (Deuteronomy 28:27, 28)

> *"You will be unsuccessful in everything you do."*
>   (Deuteronomy 28:29)

> *"You will plant a vineyard, but you will not even begin to enjoy its fruits."*   (Deuteronomy 28:30)

> *"You will have sons and daughters but you will not keep* [or enjoy] *them, because they will go into captivity."*
>   (Deuteronomy 28:41)

> *"The* Lord *will send fearful plagues on you* **and your descendants**, *harsh and prolonged disasters, and severe and lingering illnesses . . . The* Lord *will also bring on you every*

*kind of sickness and disaster not recorded in this Book of the
Law until you are destroyed."* (Deuteronomy 28:59, 61)

While society calls you a victim and the Church calls you
carnal, while Freud blames your sex drive and anthropologists
blame the culture, while psychologists argue about the relative influence of environment and heredity, the Bible talks
about generational sins and curses. According to the Word of
God, the circumstances that affect your life are directly
influenced in the spirit realm by the lifestyle of your parents
and ancestors.

Al Sanders, in his book *Crisis in Morality*, compares the
descendants of two men who lived in the United States about
150 years ago. Max Jukes was an atheist. He did not believe in
Christ or in Christian training. He married an ungodly girl
and refused to take his children to church, even when they
asked to go. At the time of this research, there were approximately 1,200 descendants from this union. Of these, 310 died
as paupers, at least 150 were criminals, 7 were murderers,
100 were drunkards, and more than half of the women were
prostitutes.

Jonathan Edwards lived at the same time as Max Jukes, but
he married a godly woman. He loved the Lord and saw that
his children were in church every Sunday as he served the
Lord to the best of his ability. An investigation was made of
1,394 of his known descendants. Thirteen of his offspring
became college presidents, 65 became college professors, 100
lawyers, 30 judges, 60 physicians, 76 army and navy officers,
100 preachers and missionaries, 60 authors of prominence,
3 United States Senators, one Vice President of the United
States, 80 public officials in other capacities, and 295 college
graduates, among whom were governors of states and ministers to foreign countries.[1]

According to some studies, as many as 92% of the people in
American prisons today were victims or witnesses of childhood abuse. Yes, heredity has played a part in their problems.
Yes, their horrendous environment influenced them toward
the path they have chosen. But, according to the Word of
God, there is another influence that no amount of human
punishment or rehabilitation can overcome: the sins of their

fathers and the resulting curses that have come upon them, which can only be broken by the cross of Jesus Christ.

Have you ever considered the validity of these Old Testament warnings in your own life? Do you have an immediate inner reaction against such a concept? Set your objections to the idea aside for just a few moments, and stay with me while we explore this together. Don't reject the possibility of generational sins and curses affecting you and your children without at least hearing everything I have to say. We will address your objections and reservations in a minute.

For now, let your imagination take you to the world in which your ancestors lived five hundred years ago. Draw out of your memory everything you know about the lifestyle of that time – the homes, the clothing, the food, the occupations, the government, the religion. Take a few minutes to immerse yourself in that era and that place. Can you see it?

Five hundred years is at least twenty generations, so it is likely that more than a million of your great-great-great-(+15 more "greats"!)-grandparents were walking around in that world you are imagining. (You have two parents, four grandparents, eight great-grandparents, sixteen great-great-grandparents, thirty-two great-great-great-grandparents, and so on.) Let's focus in on their spiritual lives. Were your ancestors from Europe? What do you think are the chances that at least one of those 1,048,576 individuals was not a worshiper of the one true God but dabbled in witchcraft or black magic? Did your family come from Africa? Do you suppose at least one of your great-grandparents may have practiced ancestor or idol worship? Are you of Asian descent? Is it possible that at least one of your forefathers was a Buddhist or Muslim? Are you Native American? Could one of your forebears have believed in pantheism or animism?

A better question might be, is it possible that any one of us has a perfect family tree in which there has never been a single person who has not served the one true God all the days of his life? I think it is highly unlikely. Yet the Lord has declared,

> *"You shall have no other gods before me. You shall not make for yourself an idol ... You shall not bow down to them or*

worship them, for I, the LORD *your God, am a jealous God,* **punishing the children for the sin of the fathers to the third and fourth generation** *of those who hate me ... "*
(Exodus 20:3–5)

"If you do not obey the LORD *your God and do not carefully follow all his commands and decrees I am giving you today, all these curses will come upon you and overtake you ...* **you will worship other gods** *– gods of wood and stone, which neither you nor your fathers have known."*
(Deuteronomy 28:15, 64)

So, five hundred years or twenty generations ago, you had an ancestor who practiced idolatry. God decreed that the punishment and the curse for that sin would last for three or four generations, and that *one of the consequences would be that the idolater's descendants would worship idols!* So generations nineteen, eighteen, seventeen and sixteen probably had at least one idol-worshiper. But great-grandma number sixteen's idolatry extended the curse down four more generations, creating idol-worshipers in generations fifteen, fourteen, thirteen and twelve, whose sin sent the curse down four more generations ... And so the cycle has continued down to you and your generation, *unless the curse has been broken!*

Sexual sins carry a similar curse, but the promise is that the consequences will influence up to the next *ten* generations! Are you sure that nowhere in your millions of ancestors there has never been any sexual immorality?

And we have only been talking about the results of the sin of one person, twenty generations ago. Multiply that exponentially by the reality of the sinful human nature that makes up your family tree, and you will see a maelstrom of generational sins and curses swirling down upon the unsuspecting and innocent heads of your children. Now double that negative sin energy, because your spouse's family tree is as diseased as yours! No wonder life is hard! No wonder there are days when we feel like we are trying to run uphill through quicksand just to stay even! No wonder we struggle so to appropriate the grace of God to overcome our sins! The channels of His grace have been dammed up by the curses of our ancestors.

I can hear you objecting: "But Jesus has redeemed us from the curse of the law by becoming a curse for us! Don't you know Galatians 3:13?"

Well, yes and no. Jesus' death on the cross paid the penalty and broke the power of sin for every member of the human race from Adam to the last man standing at the end of the age. Every single person *was saved* by Jesus' death. Yet that salvation, that forgiveness of sin and deliverance from its power, was not effective in our lives, was not applied to us, was not accounted to our behalf, until we personally accepted it by faith and appropriated it in our own lives. We must individually receive the benefits of the cross for them to be effectual for us. And *only the benefits that we personally receive by faith are effectual for us.*

Growth in the Christian life is often simply the increased revelation of what the cross of Jesus has accomplished, and the application of that revelation to our own lives. The baptism in the Holy Spirit was available to us from the moment of our salvation, but few of us received it then. The Law of the Spirit of Life in Christ Jesus was in effect as soon as He became our Lord and Savior, but few of us walked in it immediately. By His stripes we were healed, yet many of us walked in sickness even after receiving His salvation. All that is necessary for life and godliness was in the cross, yet it is not manifest in our lives until we personally receive it by faith.

The same is true of the curse of the law: Jesus has redeemed us from the curse of the law by becoming a curse for us. Absolutely. Positively. However, until we personally appropriate that redemption in our own lives, the curse still operates. When we personally take the cross of Jesus Christ and place it by faith between us and our ancestors, immediately all those generational sins and curses that have been pouring down upon us and our children come to an abrupt and absolute end. They are absorbed into the cross, for Jesus has already paid the price and suffered the penalty. Their power over us is broken because of our faith in the work of Jesus on the cross.

You can be released from the negative sin energies of your ancestors. You can live a life of freedom from the power of generational curses. You can draw freely from the wells of salvation, for the channels of God's grace can be cleared of every obstruction. Your children can start life with a clean slate, unburdened by the consequences of any sin but their own. All you must do is receive it by faith. At the end of this chapter there is a sample prayer and meditation, which I strongly encourage you to appropriate into your own life by faith. It is especially important to appropriate God's grace in this way if you have an adopted child. By the very nature of the issues that result in adoption, there is cleansing and breaking of curses that must be done.

By the grace of God, Mark and I learned about the power of generational sins and curses early in our marriage, before we had children. By faith we saw the cross of Christ standing between us and our ancestors. The sins and curses that had been bearing down upon us were absorbed into the cross. We were freed from their power! And as we stood on this side of the cross, every promise of blessing that God ever made began pouring down upon us and all future generations. When the debris of the past was cleared out, the dams blocking the channels of grace and blessing were swept away, and the flood of mercy, grace, blessing and peace that God longs for all of His children to experience began flowing freely.

The Other Side of the Cross

The negative power of sins and curses is only one aspect of the heritage that we receive from our ancestors. God's promise in Exodus 20:5–6 continues, *"I, the LORD your God, am a jealous God ... showing love to a thousand generations of those who love me and keep my commandments."*

> *"Know therefore that the LORD your God is God; he is the faithful God, keeping his **covenant of love to a thousand generations** of those who love him and keep his commands."*
> (Deuteronomy 7:9)

> *"If you fully obey the voice of the LORD your God and carefully follow all his commands I give you today, the LORD will set you high above all the nations on earth. All these blessings will come upon you and overtake you and accompany you if you*

listen to the voice of the LORD *your God. You will be blessed in the city and blessed in the country.* **The fruit of your womb will be blessed . . .** *"*   (Deuteronomy 28:1–4)

The grace and mercy of God that flow into my life and family never cease to amaze me. To the unspiritual eye, our lives appear "charmed." To the spiritual, it is clear that we are greatly blessed. Our marriage is strong. Our children are following the Lord and have never indulged in rebellious attitudes or behavior. We have a lovely home, plenty of food, more clothes than we need, and very comfortable vehicles. We have never been involved in an accident that resulted in personal injury or suffered any serious illness or disease. Mark, Charity and Joshua have all been involved in situations that could have resulted in severe injury or even death, and all have walked through without any harm coming to them. We have had the opportunity to travel all over the world, blessing and receiving blessing from our brothers and sisters in the Lord.

Often I used to look at our wonderful life and compare it to that of other sincere Christians who seemed to stagger from crisis to catastrophe. While the flu swept through their families, our family walked on in perfect health. When their new appliances broke down with distressing regularity, our old ones kept on plugging along. While they labored daily in unfulfilling dead-end jobs, we made a comfortable living doing the things we enjoyed and following a very flexible schedule. Yet their faith was as strong as ours, their devotion to the Lord as sincere as ours, their sanctification at least as great as ours. There was nothing in our lives that made us more deserving of God's blessing than they.

Finally we realized that Mark and I are walking in the blessing of a strong spiritual heritage. Both of us were raised in godly homes by truly Christian parents who lived their faith in their families as well as in public. Three of our four parents also had parents who were committed Christians. Our blessed lives today are the direct result of the godliness of our ancestors.

We have noticed a pattern among our friends who have not embraced the truth about generational sins and curses, and therefore are walking in the mixed blessings and curses into which they were born. Those of our believing friends from Christian families who married believers who also had a Christian heritage have enjoyed good lives. There have been some difficulties, but for the most part they are limited to one area of their lives at a time – either financial or physical or relational or emotional. Those who married first-generation believers, no matter how devoted and sincere, have struggled with all manner of physical, financial, emotional, church, business and family difficulties. Every step forward has been with blood, sweat and tears. Nothing has ever come to them easily.

The good news is that *no matter what heritage you received, you can pass on a godly heritage to your children and your children's children!* You can be the one who applies faith in the cross of Jesus to bring an end to the sins and curses that have plagued your family. Beginning with you, a new family tree can be planted that is strong and healthy and whose fruit is life and joy and peace to all who follow after. Your children do not have to suffer for the sins of their fathers, and neither do you! You have been redeemed from the curse of the law, and if you will diligently listen to and obey the voice of the Lord your God, blessings will run after you and chase you down in every area of your life.

> *"You will be blessed when you come in and blessed when you go out ... The Lord will send a blessing on ... everything you put your hand to ... The Lord will establish you as his holy people ... All the peoples on earth will see that you are called by the name of the Lord, and they will fear you. The Lord will grant you abundant prosperity – in the fruit of your womb, the young of your livestock and the crops of your ground ... The Lord will open the heavens, the storehouse of his bounty ... to bless all the work of your hands. You will lend to many nations but will borrow from none. The Lord will make you the head, not the tail. If you pay attention to the commands of the Lord your God and carefully follow them, you will always be at the top, never at the bottom."* (Deuteronomy 28:1–14)

> *"For no matter how many promises God has made, they are 'Yes' in Christ."* (2 Corinthians 1:20)

tage you can establish today for your children! :he slate clean, freeing them from the punish- itions past. They can enter into covenant with God without any baggage weighing them down. They can be free to make their own choices and decisions without fighting the negative sin energies of their ancestors. What great freedom you can offer your children, and with it, what great responsibility! They will never be able to use the excuse of a family weakness to justify their sin, and neither will you. You will all be able to draw on God's grace as freely and avidly as you desire. Your success and your failures will be your own.

Application and Prayer

Beginning today, you can be a better person, a better Christian, a better spouse, a better parent. Beginning at this very moment, you can be freed from the power of generational sins and curses that have influenced and harassed you all your life. The words below alone will not bring you freedom. You must speak them from your heart with faith. Read the prayer over carefully first, being sure that you understand and can wholeheartedly affirm every word. Then read it aloud prayerfully, from your heart, using the eyes of your heart to see the spiritual realities of which you speak.

> *"Lord Jesus Christ, I believe that You are the Son of God and the only way to God; and that You died on the cross for my sins and rose again from the dead.*
>
> *I give up all my rebellion and all my sin, and I submit myself to You as my Lord.*
>
> *I confess all my sins before You and ask for Your forgiveness – especially any sins that exposed me to a curse.* (As the Holy Spirit brings specific sins you have committed to your mind, draw upon His grace to truly repent and turn away from them.) *Release me also from the consequences of my ancestors' sins.*
>
> *By a decision of my will, I forgive all who have harmed me or wronged me – just as I want God to forgive me. In particular, I forgive ...* (As the Holy Spirit brings the names

or faces of people to your mind, draw upon His grace to make a decision to forgive them now.)

I renounce all contact with anything occult or satanic – if I have any "contact objects," I commit myself to destroy them. I cancel all Satan's claims against me.

Lord Jesus, I believe that on the cross You took on Yourself every curse that could ever come upon me. So I ask You now to release me from every curse over my life – in Your name, Lord Jesus Christ![2]

I place the cross of Jesus Christ between my ancestors and myself as a baby in my mother's womb. I command the sins and all accompanying curses from my ancestors to be halted at the cross of Jesus Christ, and for freedom and release to flow down from the cross to that baby in the womb. (It is most powerful to apply the grace of God at the point of need. You received the curses in your mother's womb, so that is when they should be broken. God lives in timelessness, so this is not a problem for Him. The eyes of your heart are to be used to increase your faith, so see this spiritual reality happening as you pray.)[3]

By faith I now receive my release and I thank You for it.

Lord, I now open myself to receive Your blessing in every way You want to impart it to me.[4]

Praise the Lord! He has redeemed you from the curse of the law!

Now, what about your children? If you are released, does that mean they are automatically released, also? As far as I know, there are no Scriptures that specifically answer that question, so I will tell you what I believe to be true. You must have the confirmation of the Spirit in your own heart of what you believe.

John and Paula Sandford, who teach extensively on generational sins, testify that the effects of this prayer will be manifest in all of the family members currently living and yet to be born. They believe that this is what is meant in Acts 16:31, *"Believe on the Lord Jesus Christ, and thou shalt be saved, and thy house."* The breaking of the curse by one believer can and does set free all of their family.

I concede their greater experience and wisdom. However, to

be absolutely certain that the personal sins of my children have not left any legal ground for any effects of any curses to remain, I prefer to pray with my children as well. Any children who have not yet been conceived when you receive your redemption from the curses are automatically included in your redemption, for they are still "in you" biblically speaking. However, as soon as they are conceived, the power of the curse begins working within them, and they are under its shadow. Therefore, they must be redeemed as well.

Infants and toddlers who are too young to understand anything spiritual can be redeemed by the faith of their parents. Simply pray the above prayers in faith for their release. Once a child is old enough to accept Jesus as his Lord and Savior, his level of spiritual understanding is adequate to participate with you in the prayers for his redemption. For a young child, perhaps drawing a picture of what is happening in the spiritual realm would be helpful. Older children should understand the spiritual principles, and voluntarily and wholeheartedly participate in the prayers on their behalf, personally repenting as necessary.

This general prayer of release will make a great difference in your life and the life of your family. As you continue to grow, the Holy Spirit may bring to your attention specific areas of sin in your life that have kept the door open for a curse to continue to flow to you. If that happens, simply apply the prayer once again to that specific sin and curse, and walk out in the blessings of your loving Father.

Notes

1. Resources at www.yorkcitychurch.org.uk
2. *Blessing or Curse: You Can Choose* by Derek Prince. Chosen Books, © 1990, p. 196
3. *Prayers That Heal the Heart* by Mark Virkler. Bridge-Logos Publishers, © 2000, p. 54
4. Prince, p. 197

Chapter 2

What Is Your Goal?

Have you ever built a new house? Do you remember all the excitement of planning it to be just right?

Probably you spent many hours imagining what your dream house would look like. You looked at magazines, examined builders' literature, and toured model homes. You decided what you liked and didn't like, what you could live with and what you absolutely had to have. You thought about your lifestyle and your family and your priorities, and you determined what size rooms you would need and how many.

You thought about whether you preferred a ranch or a three-story colonial. You laid out the floor plan to be most convenient for the way you do things. You decided how many bathrooms you wanted, and where the major appliances would stand. You thought about your hobbies and interests, and decided whether the workbench would be in the basement or the garage. Before the first survey stake was placed in the ground, you probably could have described your completed house in great detail.

Once you made all of these decisions, and countless more, you explained all of your goals to your architect. It was absolutely necessary that he have a complete understanding of how the finished building was to look and be used before he could draw up the plans and specifications needed to create that final result.

A cement slab foundation might hold a small ranch, but you would need a good strong basement for that three-story of your dreams. The need for adequate weight-bearing walls might require some adjusting of your floor plan. Proper electrical wiring and breakers had to be installed in the right places to service appliances and power tools. The heating/air conditioning/humidifier system had to be carefully chosen and properly installed to ensure comfort in every room.

The number of people you planned to accommodate would determine the size of the septic system. The plumbing would need to be routed and sized appropriately. The climate of the area in which you were building would need to be factored in to the decision on amount and type of insulation needed. And would your building need to withstand hurricanes or tornadoes or earthquakes? That would bring in a whole new set of specifications.

So many decisions to be made just to get the supporting structure right. And you haven't even begun with the decorating! I imagine you spent many hours talking, studying, debating and learning more than you ever really wanted to know about construction. But it is totally understandable. Buying a house is the single greatest financial investment most couples make during their lives. You want to be certain that every decision you make contributes to the outcome you desire.

I wonder how many of us have spent a comparable amount of time considering the "finished product" we desire from our investment in raising children. What exactly are we hoping to accomplish, anyway? What indicators will attest to our success? What behaviors and attitudes do we want to see in our preschoolers? What does a "good" elementary child look like? Is there such a thing as a high quality teenager? When our job is finished (if it ever really is), what kind of adults do we want our offspring to be?

Have you thought at all about what God expects of you as a parent? Have you assumed that raising children is an instinctive ability – people do it all the time, so what's the big deal? You turned out pretty good so you'll just raise your kids the way your parents raised you. What's to think about or pray about or study about?

If we don't know where we are going, any road will do. And if we have no specific, definite goal toward which we are aiming in our child rearing, any philosophy and method-ology is acceptable. It doesn't matter what "expert" we listen to, or if we listen to anyone. It doesn't matter how we nurture, train and discipline. But, if we do have a specific goal, then we must carefully choose the methods, techniques, and attitudes that will advance our children toward that target.

Even if we haven't consciously developed a goal for our children, we most likely have unconscious ideas about the purpose of parenting and the place of children. Let's look at some of them.

"Don't Embarrass Me!"

Bart and Barbie Blusher hold to the old saw that children are to be seen and not heard. Their highest ambition is that their children not embarrass them in any way. "Just don't make us look bad!" is their mantra. They live in mortal fear of toddler temper tantrums in the grocery store, sibling arguments in the restaurant, and unwed teen pregnancies.

Bart and Barbie believe the best way to achieve their goal is to impose endless rules with strong consequences. Every activity and every relationship is controlled by its governing regulations. Barbie's most common form of communication is nagging, and Bart's is lecturing. Junior Blushers are allowed little freedom of expression, and punishment for stepping out of line is swift and severe. Teenage Blushers who dare to taint the image Bart and Barbie try to maintain are no longer welcome in the "home" and may find themselves out on the street.

"Make Me Look Good!"

Bob and Bonnie Braggin, on the other hand, expect their children to make them look good. They need the validation they feel from the successes of their offspring. Bonnie can tell you to the minute how old the children were when they began to walk and talk, and Bob loves to recount their latest achieve-ments. There is no leisure time in the Braggin household, for every moment of every day is tightly scheduled with enriching activities. The annual Braggin Christmas letter waxes eloquent with the details of the lessons and activities, awards and honors the children have enjoyed. Like the Blushers, Bob and Bonnie also resort to strict legalism to accomplish their goal. Little Braggins' personal interests and desires are ignored as they are pressured to glowingly reflect their parents' superiority.

"Fulfill My Dreams!"

Ben Brokin was the captain of his high school football team and received a full athletic scholarship to a great college. His future looked bright as a professional player, enjoying wealth and fame and prestige for years to come. It all came crashing down when he blew out his knee in the championship game. The scholarship was withdrawn, and all of his dreams dissolved into dust, with no hope of affording college without it. Angry and resentful, he settled for a blue-collar job he hated but stuck with for the rest of his life.

His wife Betty knows something about lost dreams herself. From the very first time she saw Swan Lake on PBS when she was only four years old, she knew she was destined to be a prima ballerina. Free lessons at the church and the YMCA taught her the basics, but the time came when she needed professional training. Unfortunately, her single mom couldn't squeeze out the extra money needed for lessons, and Betty watched her dreams fade away.

When little Babs was born, Betty determined that nothing was going to keep her from being all that she herself had longed to be. She started ballet classes at the most prestigious dance school in town when she was only two, with private lessons every summer. Wherever she goes, Babs is dressed in ribbons and lace, looking every inch the feminine doll of her mother's dreams. Unfortunately, Babs hasn't been interested in dancing since she "helped" her daddy tune the car when she was seven. Now she would rather spend a day tearing apart the lawnmower in her baggy, grease-covered sweats than five minutes doing stretches in her tutu. But Betty doesn't want to hear about her dreams and interests, clinging blindly to her own ideas of what makes a young girl happy.

Young Benny isn't faring much better. With his mother's slender build, everyone but his dad recognizes that sports will never be his forte. Big Ben is convinced that all he needs is more weight training to build up those muscles and he will be a terror on the field. Football camps every summer, practices after school, and strenuous workouts with his bullying father on the weekends haven't made any noticeable improvement in his game. Nor has his father's mockery of "computer geeks" diminished his passion for programming. Instead, they have only strengthened the resentment and rebellion seething in his heart, and his resolve to get out of this house as soon as he can.

Ben and Betty treat their children as if they were carbon copies of themselves, not seeing their unique personalities and gifts. As a result, they run roughshod over them, crushing their spirits and allowing their potential to go unrealized.

"Be Like Me!"

Bill and Bitsy Beemee were a lot like Big Ben Brokin. They reached their pinnacle of success in high school. Those were the glory days when they were popular, the life of every party, head cheerleader and captain of the football team. Unfortunately, life since then has not been as kind as it promised it would be, and today they view their youth through the rose-colored shades of remembered happiness.

Like Ben and Betty Brokin who want their children to fulfill their broken dreams, Bill and Bitsy also try to force their children into their idea of a perfect childhood. They believe that the things that made them happy in their youth will also make their children happy. If their children will only do what they did, act as they acted, live as they lived, they, too, will have a perfect childhood. The activities that brought them popularity and temporary success in their youth are still the key to vicarious popularity and success today, through the lives of their offspring.

They are unsympathetic to the stresses of being a young person today, belittling any complaint of pressure with stories

of the joys of the "good old days." They are not concerned about supporting their children's interests, pressuring
them instead to pursue the activities in which they found
fulfillment.

"Be a Believer!"

Brian and Brianna Betterway recognized early their own self-
centered tendencies as parents and gladly surrendered them
to their Lord. They see their children not as extensions of
themselves but as gifts from God over whom He has given
them stewardship for a short time.

They took the salvation of their children as their overriding
goal, and were deeply blessed to lead each of their children to
the Lord at an early age. The entire family is active in church,
attending all the services and volunteering in many ministries. They have had some rough patches and experienced
some "normal teenage rebellion," but they cling to the
promise of Proverbs 22:6 and have faith that, though there
may be a period when their children stray from the Lord,
when they are old they will surely return.

What about You?

Do you recognize yourself in any of our fictional friends?
What are you aiming for?

Stephen Covey asserts that one of *The 7 Habits of Highly
Effective People* is to "Begin with the end in mind." What do
you have in mind for your children? What do you want God
to say about you as a parent?

If you have not already done so, I strongly encourage you to
take the time *now* to define the goals you have for your
children. Seek the Lord's will, and make it your will. And once
you know His goal, seek His direction for how to accomplish it.
What will you need to do to train your children as He desires?
What must your attitudes be toward their interests, personalities, goals, gifts, and weaknesses? What kind of discipline will
be most effective in shaping their behavior without crushing
their spirits? What kind of parent must you be in order to
produce the next generation that God has in mind?

As for Me and My House . . .

In the rest of this chapter I want to share with you the goal the Lord gave us for our children, and what that meant to our child-rearing techniques.

When it comes right down to it, life is all about making decisions. Every aspect of our lives involves making choices, deciding which of all the available options is best in this particular situation. From the (apparently) mundane, daily decisions about what to eat and what to wear to the life-transforming choices about who to marry and what profession to pursue, from the insignificant decisions about which household chore to tackle first on our day off to the character-shaping choices involving honesty and integrity – every day is a parade of decisions we must make, and every life is a result of the decisions we have made. Therefore, the ability to make wise decisions has been our number one goal for our children.

> *"The father of the righteous will greatly rejoice,*
> *And he who sires a wise son will be glad in him.*
> *Let your father and your mother be glad,*
> *And let her rejoice who gave birth to you."*
>
> (Proverbs 23:24, 25)

The most effective way we know to help someone learn to make good decisions is to allow him to make as many decisions as possible, and, when appropriate, allow him to experience the consequences of his decisions. That means that we encouraged our children to begin making choices and decisions from a very early age.

For example, a daily choice was what to wear. At first, I would offer them a choice of two possible outfits that were appropriate for the occasion, and allow their decision to be final. As they grew a bit older, their clothes were sorted by occasion: play clothes, nice casual clothes (for outings to the library or store), and dressy, Sunday clothes. I told them which group to choose from and they were allowed to choose whatever they wanted. This made for some rather colorful and interesting combinations on occasion, to be sure! But positive reinforcement was effective in gradually guiding them to more traditional ensembles.

Other choices they were encouraged to make included which vegetable to serve for dinner, which household chore to do on which day of the week, which books to borrow from the library, which school subjects to tackle first, what electives to study for the coming school year, which restaurant to go to, what to do on days off, where to go on vacations ... there were an infinite number of decisions that could safely be left to our children.

Naturally, that doesn't mean that we simply said, "Choose" and left them to their own devices. We would talk together about the benefits and drawbacks of each possibility, clarifying any positive or negative consequences they would be assuming by their decision.

And Mark and I discussed many of our own decisions in front of, or with, the children. We let them see us interacting with the problem and each other, modeling our method of coming to a decision. As they grew older, we spent time specifically teaching them what we call "The Leader's Paradigm for Decision-Making," the philosophy behind our methodology. (See Appendix A.) We always encouraged them to talk over their questions and decisions with us, and we always tried to be clear-headed and objective in our input.

Of course, the examples of decisions I have given so far are quite easily delegated to children. The consequences of a wrong choice are relatively minor and painless. The test of our commitment to training our children in wisdom comes when they face the more serious challenges of friendship, morality and integrity. How should they respond to the neighborhood bully? How do they react when their friends begin to harass the eccentric elderly shop owner? What is their response to the pressure of their peers to mock the less attractive, cheat on the math test, steal from the corner store, have a little drink, try a little pot, enjoy a little sexual pleasure? Just because your child accepted Jesus into her heart when she was four, will she be ready and able to face the temptations of adolescence with strength and purity?

Our true goal as Christian parents is therefore not simply that our children make wise decisions. Frankly, we are not interested in the decisions even the wisest human mind can make. We are those who "do nothing on [our] own initiative." We do not seek our own will but the will of our Father who sent us (John 5:30). We do not seek earthly human wisdom, but the wisdom that is from above, that is full of good fruits (James 3:15–18). We want only those thoughts that are so much higher than our human thoughts, and the ways that are so much higher than our human ways (Isaiah 55:8,9). Therefore, our goal is not that our children make wise decisions based on their own insights and abilities, but that *they recognize God's voice for themselves and live always and only out of His voice and His vision and His initiative.*

We were not satisfied to simply lead our children to the Lord when they were young and then expect their Sunday school teachers to fill their spiritual needs. We were called to disciple our children, to encourage them to follow us as we follow Christ. It was our responsibility to bring them not only to physical maturity but also to social, emotional, and spiritual maturity. To us, that meant training them to personally hear God's voice within their own hearts and live in obedience to Him. If a child is old enough to hear the Holy Spirit calling Him to repentance and salvation, he is old enough to hear the Holy Spirit guiding him on a daily basis.

That means that leading your child to Christ is not your ultimate goal but only your first step. Do you believe that the Holy Spirit takes up residence in a believer when he is born again? Do you believe He lives within the young child just as He lives within the adult? Is God's grace and ability limited by the age of the one who comes to Him in faith? Would you be as slow to recognize that God was speaking to your child as Eli was to identify God's voice for Samuel? Are you confident in *your* ability to hear God's voice within your own heart? Are you able to teach your children how they can recognize the voice of the Spirit within them? Are you prepared for them to submit what they hear to you for confirmation and adjustment, based on what you have also heard from God?

Jesus welcomed the children who came to Him, declaring that His kingdom is made up of those who receive Him in childlike faith and trust. Essentially, He was saying that children naturally have the abilities necessary to be part of

His kingdom. Any time we make a part of Christianity too difficult or beyond the reach of children, we have perverted the simplicity of the Gospel and are no longer messengers of the Good News.

Children can and must be born again, some even as young as three or four years old. But that is just the beginning! Once the Holy Spirit is living within them, they can and must learn how to recognize His conviction, His guidance, His wisdom – His voice within them leading them into all truth and right-eousness. This is the greatest channel of grace we can open up for our children – the ability to hear and the desire to obey the voice of the Lord within their own hearts! If we will cultivate this ability, if we will train our children to recognize the Holy Spirit's presence and power within them from the very day of their salvation, He Who began a good work in them will carry it on to completion (Philippians 1:6 NIV)!

It is not our responsibility as parents to control the actions of our saved children. It is our responsibility as disciplers to instruct them in the Scriptures and help them personally get to know the One Who is at work *within them* both to will and to do His good pleasure (Philippians 2:13 KJV). It is the *grace* of God that not only brings salvation but which teaches us, *and will teach our children*, to say "No" to ungodliness and worldly passions, and to live self-controlled, upright and godly lives in this present age (Titus 2:11, 12 NIV).

It is so tempting to place our children, who have been saved by grace just as we were, back under the Law. (What am I talking about? It is tempting for us to put ourselves and everyone else we know back under the Law!) It has been a temptation that believers have faced since the days of Paul. But the Law will no more justify or sanctify your children than it could justify or sanctify the Galatians.

It is not enough to teach your children the rules: "Good Christians don't use those words. Good little girls don't sass their mommies. Good little boys don't hit their sisters. You'll make God sad if you don't go to Sunday school. God wants you to do this. God doesn't want you to do that." That is just attempting to justify them by the Law, which Paul says will alienate them from Christ and cause them to *fall away from grace* (Galatians 5:4). It is for freedom that Christ has set them free. It is not our responsibility or even our right to burden them with the Law – not God's Law and especially not our own laws. Instead, we must teach them to live by the Spirit and then they *will not* gratify the desires of the flesh (Galatians 5:16).

The Place of the Law

Am I saying, then, that there were no laws or rules in our house? Of course not. The Law is for those who are not under grace, which includes both those who are not yet born again and those who are born again but are not living in obedience to the voice of the Lord through the *logos* (God's Word written in the Scriptures) and *rhema* (God's Word spoken in the heart). So until your children come into a personal relationship with the Lord, they must live under commandments, statutes, rules and laws.

(In Deuteronomy 5:22–33, Moses recounts the sad story of the Israelites' refusal to live in relationship with God for fear of the darkness and the fire that accompanied His Presence. As a result, they had to live under commandments and statutes and judgments. The only alternative to relationship is rules.)

However, I really want to encourage you to think carefully before you establish any rule in your home. Excessive, superfluous, irrational, unnecessary rules have no place in the Christian home. Your goal is to lead them to Christ, not incite rebellion. And unexplainable rules *will* lead to rebellion.

According to Romans 7:5, laws can have an even more detrimental effect on the unbeliever: *"For while we were in the flesh, the sinful passions, **which were aroused by the Law**, were at work in the members of our body to bear fruit for death."* The very rules that you make can stir up the desire within your unsaved children to do things they would have had no interest in had there been no rule against it. The forbidden fruit always looks most enticing.

Don't establish a rule just because it was a rule in your house when you were a child. Be sure in your own heart that it is a rule God wants established in the home in which you are a parent. Don't be pressured by the prevailing theories being presented in your church or other social environments. Hear God's guidance for you yourself, in concert with your spouse. If you can't reasonably defend a rule, strongly consider rejecting it.

I have never been a big fan of the "Because I said so and that's all the reason you need!" approach to explanations, either. I admit that there were a few occasions of stress and fatigue that did result in those words coming from my mouth, but I tried to resist the temptation as much as possible. Safety and courtesy issues are the foundation of most necessary rules, and most children will accept a simple explanation of them. Of course, a child does not need to accept the explanation to be required to obey the rule, but it usually will promote greater cooperation.

It seems to me that too often we simply pass on the rules we have heard all our lives without really examining their usefulness or necessity. Always being ready to give an explanation stimulates you to weed out those secondhand, worn-out regulations.

For example, give a child a glass of chocolate milk and he will drink it, no problem. Now, put a straw in that glass of milk and what is his immediate response? He will blow bubbles, of course! I don't know what it is about straws in milk, but rare is the child that can resist this temptation. And rare is the parent who can resist the temptation to immediately say, "Don't blow bubbles in your milk!" Yet, what is wrong with it, really? Particularly when you are at home in a casual setting with just your family, what is the problem with blowing bubbles in your milk? It's fun. It doesn't hurt anyone. As long as care is taken not to run over the top of the glass, why shouldn't he indulge in a little harmless bubbling?

There are many other similar regulations that we impose on children that seem pointless and unnecessary. I strongly urge you to hear from God concerning every standard of behavior that you establish for your home and family. According to Galatians 3:23–25, rules and regulations should serve one of two purposes: to keep us safe and pure until we come to faith in Christ, or to reveal Christ to us, drawing us into a relationship with Him.

"But before faith came, we were kept under guard by the law, kept for the faith which would afterward be revealed. Therefore the law was our tutor to bring us to Christ, that we might be justified by faith. But after faith has come, we are no longer under a tutor." (NKJV)

The Place of Corporal Punishment

I have always been ambivalent concerning spanking children. We did occasionally spank our children but for me, it was usually either because of my own fatigue or frustration or because the books I had read on parenting decreed that such punishment was necessary in those circumstances. But I have never really felt right about hitting a child.

The usual text given in support of corporal punishment is Proverbs 22:15,

"Foolishness is bound in the heart of a child; but the rod of correction shall drive it far from him." (KJV)

However, I would like you to consider the significance of the promise of Ezekiel 36:26, 27:

*"A **new heart** also will I give you, and a new spirit will I put within you: and I will take away the stony heart out of your flesh, and I will give you an heart of flesh. And I will put my spirit within you, and cause you to walk in my statutes, and ye shall keep my judgments, and do them."* (KJV)

Our born again children no longer have a heart that is full of foolishness. They have been given a new heart on which is written the Law of God. A rod of correction is no longer necessary to cleanse their hearts, for the Spirit of Christ has already done so!

Ask the Lord for His wisdom and direction in how He wants you to discipline both your born again and your not-yet-born-again children. Only what is done out of the voice and vision of God will bear eternal fruit.

The Law and Grace

Because our children were saved, filled with the Holy Spirit, and learned to hear the voice of God for themselves at a young age, the rules of our home were not a high standard toward which they had to strive. Instead, they were the minimum acceptable behavior. They were not a goal toward which they struggled, but a safety net to catch them should they forget or choose not to obey the voice of the Lord within them.

For example, hitting, slapping, pinching, biting – all physical violence against one another was against the law of our household. There could also be no name-calling or cruel words of any kind. My preference was that there would be no verbal fights, but my sisters and I fought a lot when we were young so I assumed that was unavoidable. However, when there was a disagreement between the children, I asked them each what Jesus wanted them to do. By encouraging them to seek the Lord's will for themselves and draw on His grace to live as He wanted them to, they developed the ability to get along with each other. Arguments became more and more rare, and physical fights were nearly unheard of. They learned to be sensitive to the feelings of others, and to honor and cooperate with the inherent differences between males and females. They became and continue to be the best of friends and confidantes. Legalism could keep them from hurting each other; grace united them in love.

I had always tried to feed my family healthy food and limit empty calories and junk food intake. There were therefore household rules about eating the vegetables before dessert and limiting between-meal snacks. However, when Charity was about fifteen and Joshua thirteen, Mark faced a potentially serious health issue, which led him to research the effects of diet on health and longevity. Each day he would share with us what he was learning and we would discuss how the Lord wanted us to respond to the new knowledge we were gaining.

We were led to adopt a very restricted vegan (no animal products at all) diet for a short time to allow our bodies to cleanse themselves of the effects of years of abuse. We then settled into a more varied diet that is largely vegetarian with occasional indulgences in meat. We cut back on sweets to just one or two days a week. Because that was the way I shopped and cooked, that became the law of the household.

However, Charity (who had by this time been journaling – writing her conversations with God – for seven years) was led to hold a higher standard. Because she regularly participated in short-term missions, the Lord told her it was important that she take special care of her body so it would be able to face the demands of the field. She was therefore to live as a strict vegetarian, eating no meat, poultry or fish, which she has done since she was sixteen. In addition, she has eaten very little chocolate or sweets, and maintains a rigorous exercise routine. Again, because she heard from the Lord for herself and drew on His grace to obey, she keeps the "law" and goes far beyond it.

Mark and I personally are teetotalers who never drink alcohol. It was the way we were raised and it has never been an issue for us. We have never felt the need to develop a taste for strong drink, and in fact our drink of choice is water. However, we do not find biblical support for such a position, but rather see prohibitions only against drunkenness. We therefore did not impose any rules against drinking upon our kids, although it was discussed and they knew our personal opposition to it.

Joshua's best friend was raised in a Christian family who are social drinkers. Since he reached legal age, parties and meals have always included wine, beer or mixed drinks. Joshua is also of legal age and has had plenty of opportunities to indulge if he chose. However, in his study of Scripture, he discovered the following passage:

> *"It is not for kings, O Lemuel –*
> *not for kings to drink wine,*
> *not for rulers to crave beer,*
> *lest they drink and forget what the law decrees,*
> *and deprive all the oppressed of their rights.*
> *Give beer to those who are perishing,*
> *wine to those who are in anguish;*
> *let them drink and forget their poverty*
> *and remember their misery no more."*
>
> (Proverbs 31:4–7 NIV)

Because the Lord has called him to be a leader one day, he has chosen not to make strong drink a part of his life. What the law might not accomplish, grace is more than able to achieve.

Although we were not thrilled with the concept of dating and the physical involvement that so often accompanies it, Mark and I accepted the "reality" that it was part of the culture in which we live and a necessary part of the process of finding a mate. However, we made the rule that there would be no dating until the kids were sixteen, and no touching anything that is covered by a swimsuit. We also spent plenty of time discussing the temptations and pitfalls of touching, petting, and physical intimacy long before they reached their sixteenth birthdays.

During Chari's and Josh's teen years, the concept of courting began to be taught in homeschool circles. They were challenged by Ron Luce at Teen Mania's Acquire the Fire to set themselves apart from romantic relationships and "date God" for a year. Chastity and purity were encouraged on many fronts. As a result of the teaching they heard and their personal conversations with the Lord, they both independently decided not to seek romantic dating relationships but to wait for the Lord to bring their mate into their lives, and to refrain from kissing until they are engaged. Charity received a "promise ring" for her sixteenth birthday and continues to wear it to demonstrate to everyone interested that she is set apart to the Lord and her future husband. I would not have even tried to impose these laws on them, but grace leads them to a higher standard than the law ever could.

I so much want to encourage you to raise your believing, Christian children in grace! Yes, there can be rules, but they are only there as a safety net to catch them from plunging to disaster if they fall out of grace. Legalism leads to resentment and rebellion, and away from the necessity to personally hear God and rely on His grace daily. How often have we heard of children from strict legalistic homes who go crazy when they get their first taste of freedom at college? Why does this happen? They know all the rules – why don't they follow them when there is no one there to enforce them? It is because the rules have been imposed from the outside rather than birthed from the inside. They are the standards of other people, not their own convictions.

Tommy Tyson has stated, "Christianity is an inside job" – the Holy Spirit works from inside us, rather than through an imposition of law from without. It is as we love others, including our own children, with the love of Christ which is absolute, does not judge or place conditions, that the Holy Spirit is free to change them from within according to His power and grace.

Remember the promise of the new covenant that the writer of Hebrews quoted in chapter 8:10–11:

> *"For this is the covenant that I will make with the House of Israel after those days, says the Lord:* **I will put my laws into their minds, and I will write them on their hearts.** *And I will be their God, and they shall be my people. And they shall not teach everyone his fellow citizen, and everyone his brother saying, 'Know the Lord,' for all will know me,* **from the least to the greatest of them."**

What a glorious promise we have been given! God Himself will write His laws on the minds and hearts of His children, and that includes *our* believing children. Our responsibility is to be obedient to Deuteronomy 6:6–9:

> *"These words, which I am commanding you today, shall be on* **your** *heart. You shall teach them diligently to your sons and shall talk of them when you sit in your house and when you walk by the way and when you lie down and when you rise up. You shall bind them as a sign on your hand and they shall be as frontals on your forehead. You shall write them on the doorposts of your house and on your gates."*

We must diligently teach the written Word of God to our children in word and in deed. Our conversation should be saturated with principles from the Scriptures. When we are driving in the car we should be sharing what the Lord has been teaching us through our meditation on the Word and in our journaling. We should be discussing our dreams and the interpretation God has given us over the breakfast table, exploring together the ways in which God is healing and leading us.

His words should be bound as a sign on our hands – all that we put our hands to do should be a reflection of His commandments and principles. They should be as frontals on our foreheads – every thought taken captive to the obedience of Christ (2 Corinthians 10:5). They should be written on the doorposts and gates of our homes – - the final authority and source of all wisdom and knowledge.

As our believing children grow in their knowledge of the Scriptures, their ability to recognize the pure *rhema* word of God in their hearts will also increase. Daily they will grow in grace and in the knowledge of their Lord and Savior, Jesus Christ.

The End of the Law

It is true that you can control the behavior of your children through strict and extensive rules. You can make your children act like good Christians and give the appearance of obedient submission.

We have a friend with an adopted son whose spirit of rejection gradually became manifest in disobedience and rebellion as he grew older. Knowing nothing about deliverance, inner healing or the breaking of generational curses, our friends focused on dealing with the outward behavioral symptoms rather than the internal underlying causes of his problems. Finally, in desperation, they sent him to military school when he was thirteen years old. Law and discipline became the only forces in his life. His behavior was brought under control, but at what cost? His face is now an expressionless mask, cold and hard beyond his fourteen years. His actions have been restrained but his spirit has been crushed. The letter has indeed brought death (2 Corinthians 3:6).

Controlling the behavior of your children must not be your goal. You must aim higher! You should be satisfied with nothing less than your children having such a close personal relationship with their Lord that they know exactly what He is doing and saying in each situation and are able to draw upon His grace to say and do only the same.

Knowing a Voice or Knowing the Person?

When we began our search to know the voice of God, we ignorantly believed that was all we needed. Rather like recognizing the voice of the President of the United States when we tuned the radio to the right station, we would be able to tune to the right "wavelength" to home in on God's voice whenever we needed direction and instruction.

We discovered, however, that God wanted us to recognize His voice so He could build a relationship with us. He didn't want us to just "tune in" when we wanted or needed something from Him. He wanted us to have a continuous, on-going communion with Him that would lead us into a deep, intimate knowledge of one another. This rapport between us is one of the great channels by which His grace pours into our lives.

Second Peter 1:2–7 says:

> *"Grace and peace be multiplied to you in the **knowledge** of God and of Jesus our Lord; seeing that His divine power has granted to us everything pertaining to life and godliness, through the true **knowledge** of Him who called us by His own glory and excellence. For by these He has granted to us His precious and magnificent promises, so that by them you may become partakers of the divine nature, having escaped the corruption that is in the world by lust. Now for this very reason also, applying all diligence, in your faith supply moral excellence, and in your moral excellence, knowledge, and in your knowledge, self-control, and in your self-control, perseverance, and in your perseverance, godliness, and in your godliness, brotherly kindness, and in your brotherly kindness, love."*

God's grace will be multiplied to us and to our children as we grow in the knowledge of God and Jesus our Lord. The word for "knowledge" (highlighted above) means the most intimate knowing of the union of a husband and wife. It is this deep bond of love and understanding between our Lord and us that opens the channels of grace that provide us with all we need for life and godliness. It is by their real, actual,

day-by-day association with Jesus that our children increase
in moral excellence, self-control, godliness, brotherly kindness and love. It is by their daily communion with God that
they have access to the grace whereby they become holy!

Where Do I Start?

If you want to raise your children to live out of the voice of
God, under grace and not law, your first step must be to be
sure that you are able to recognize the Lord's voice within
your own heart and that you are living in obedience to Him.
Jesus has promised that His sheep hear His voice, so if you are
His sheep, you are hearing His voice. The challenge in our
twenty-first century world is confidently distinguishing His
voice from among the babble of voices that try to claim your
attention each day. If you are not confidently able to say,
"The Lord told me ... ," I encourage you to seek out instruction that will bring you to that place in your Christian life.
Refer to the Bibliography for books that may be helpful to
you, and see Appendix B for a summary of four keys to
hearing God's voice.

Once you are confident in your ability to recognize your
Lord's voice, you are ready to bring your children into the
same exciting experience. Of course, the prerequisite to
hearing God within is inviting Him to live within. So you
want to lead your children to Christ as soon as possible. A
deep theological understanding of soteriology is not necessary – just a sorrow for their sins and a desire to follow Jesus.
This can come at a very young age – many missionaries testify
to receiving Christ when they were only three or four years
old.

When your children accept Jesus as their Lord and Savior,
explain to them that the Holy Spirit is now living within
them. It is He Who lets them know deep inside, within their
spirit, that they are now God's children (Romans 8:16). It is
He Who will lead them into all truth (John 16:13). It is He
Who is working in them to will and to act according to His
good purpose (Philippians 2:13). And it is He Who will
sanctify them, setting them apart for God and making them
holy through and through (1 Thessalonians 5:23). Therefore

they should begin listening immediately to the new voice that they will hear within them after they ask Jesus into their hearts.

It will probably be easier for your children to hear the Lord than it is for you because they won't have the years of rationalistic, humanistic indoctrination that you have received in our western culture. If they are immediately encouraged to honor the voice within them, their senses will never become dull and they will have the privilege of living under grace throughout their lives. Refer to the Bibliography for recommendations of books to help you gain confidence in leading your child to the Lord and guiding him in recognizing his Lord's voice within him.

WWJD?

In recent years, the "WWJD?"phenomenon has been sweeping through Christianity. Bible covers, t-shirts, and jewelry all bear the question "WWJD?" Mark and I both read *In His Steps* by Charles Sheldon when we were young and were also inspired by the idea of asking ourselves, "What would Jesus do?" when we needed to make a decision. I respect the sincerity of those who have taken up this challenge. In fact, you may think what I have recommended above is just a variation on this idea. Actually, I have at least two major problems with the WWJD? question, and want to make the distinction between the two approaches very clear.

First of all, I don't believe we have a clue what Jesus would do in any given situation! His ways are not our ways and His thoughts are not our thoughts! He was forever doing the unexpected and confounding both His disciples and His enemies. We simply are not able *with our own minds* to figure out what Jesus would do. Even if we were to think of a Scripture verse that seemed to apply to our situation, chances are good that the verse we chose would not be the one that Jesus would apply.

Let's imagine a day in the life of a devoted Christian worker (we'll call her Sally) who is trying to remember to live according to the answers she gets to the question, "What would Jesus do?"

It's Sunday morning, so Sally arrives at church early to prepare for the Sunday school class of Juniors she teaches. She greets each one individually and soon the class is engrossed in a lively discussion of the lesson. Suddenly there is a knock at the door. Little Johnny runs over, flings it open with a flourish, and calls over his shoulder, "Hey Teacher! It's your mom! She wants to talk to you!" Sally hates to break up the flow of the lesson, but she can't ignore her mom. What would Jesus do? Of course! It's a "no-brainer." There's even a Scripture verse: *"Honor your father and mother."* Right?

Wrong! When Jesus was faced with this situation, He remained where He was and essentially negated the special relationship His mother had with Him, making it equal with that of any of His disciples (Matthew 12:46–50).

After church, Sally takes her class for a picnic down by the lake. They can't help overhearing a young mother struggling with her obstreperous daughter at a nearby table, but they try to ignore the disturbance. After lunch, they begin to sing songs about Jesus. The children take turns calling out their favorites and a spirit of praise and worship falls upon them. The presence of the Lord is truly in that place. Suddenly, during a moment of silence, Sally feels a tap on her arm. It is the young mother standing there with tears running down her face. Standing quietly by her side is her daughter, now calm and controlled.

"Please, can you help me?" the woman asks Sally in a strongly accented voice. "I don't know what is wrong with my little girl. Something just comes over her and it's as if she were not even herself when she becomes so wild and unreasonable. The children with you are so different, and I feel like you have something that could help me."

What would Jesus do? Of course, He would immediately minister to this needy family. After all, He went about doing good and healing all those who were oppressed of the devil (Acts 10:38). Right?

Wrong! Though it may bother us to imagine the scene, in a similar situation Jesus first ignored, and then actually insulted the woman, calling her a dog, and refusing to minister deliverance to her child (Matthew 15:21–28). (Of course, her faith was such that He relented and did minister to her after all.)

A little while later, the sky begins to darken and clouds form across the lake. Sally takes the opportunity to dramatize for her class the story of Jesus calming the storm. They listen raptly, unaware that other picnickers have gathered around the edge of their group to listen as well. As she draws to a climax, she is interrupted by a loud voice, "You don't really believe all that garbage do you? Why are you filling these kids' heads with such nonsense? You shouldn't be allowed to brainwash them with your old-fashioned, out-dated, ignorant old wives' tales!"

What would Jesus do? *"Bless them that curse you." "A soft answer turns away wrath."* Right?

Wrong! When confronted by the hostile ignorance of the unbelievers of His day, Jesus called them whitewashed tombs, looking good on the outside but full of death on the inside (Matthew 23:27). Not the best way to win friends and influence people!

Gradually the crowd disperses and Sally begins to gather her brood together to head home. That's when she notices a man leaning against a nearby tree. His white cane identifies him as blind, so before she leaves the area, she stops to ask if there is anything she can do for him. "I want to see!" he responds passionately. "I heard your story. I believe in Jesus, too, and I believe He did miracles when He walked on earth. Do you think He still heals today?" Her class has huddled around them as they talked, and now they turn their eager faces up to her. "Yes!" they cry. "Jesus will heal him! We know He will!"

What would Jesus do? Of course He would want to heal this child of His. But what should you do? *"Is any sick among you? Let them call for the elders of the church and let them pray over them, anointing them with oil. . . . . . "* (James 5:14, 15). So, Sally concludes, she should take the blind man back to her church where the pastor and elders can pray for his healing. Right?

Wrong! Jesus healed blindness a different way every time He faced it. He cast demons out of one. He laid His hands on another. The most unexpected thing He did was to spit on the ground, stir it into mud with His finger, and then rub it on the blind eyes (John 9:6)! What would Jesus do? Who knows?!

The twenty-first century Church has developed a picture of "lowly Jesus, meek and mild" that is often quite different from the Jesus we see if we really read the Scripture. Jesus was always doing the unexpected, the unacceptable, the irreligious thing! We cannot possibly think up with our own little minds what Jesus would do in our situation. It is impossible. If we ask ourselves, "What would Jesus do?" chances are excellent that the answer we come up with will be totally wrong.

My second problem with the question, "What would Jesus do?" is the unspoken yet understood conditional clause that follows it: *"if He were here!"* The implied underlying assumption of "WWJD?" is that Jesus is not here today, and I take strong exception to this supposition. My Jesus *is* here today, and He is still actively moving and accomplishing His will. Therefore, my question is not, "What *would* Jesus do?" but "What *is* Jesus doing?" I want to follow Jesus' example Who did nothing except what He saw the Father doing and said nothing except what He heard the Father saying. I want to know what Jesus and the Father and the Spirit are doing *right now*, and I want to be a part of it.

This is a significant distinction. WWJD depends on my memory of Scripture, my ability to choose the right verse for each situation, and my intellect to figure out, from what I know about Jesus, how He would react in the situation. WIJD (What is Jesus doing?) depends upon my ability to see into the spirit with the eyes of my heart what Jesus is presently doing, and hear with my spiritual ears what He is presently saying. WWJD will lead to legalism, while WIJD will lead to grace. They are our only two options: If we do not live out of His voice, we are forced to live under the Law (Deuteronomy 5:22–33).

Are You Ready?

Are you prepared to lead your child to Christ? If you are unconvinced of your adequacy in Him to do so yourself, do you provide plenty of opportunities for him to hear the Gospel and be presented with the need to make a personal decision? Have you talked with your child about his relationship with Jesus? What does the Holy Spirit want to do through you to help your child take her next step in Christ?

Are you confident in your ability to recognize the Lord's voice? Do you have daily communion with Him? Is His grace being multiplied in you as you grow in your knowledge of Him? If not, what does the Holy Spirit want you to do about this lack in your life?

Are you able to explain to your children how they can hear God's voice and develop an intimate relationship with Him? Have you talked with them about how much He wants to chat with them about their lives every day? Have you shared your growth in grace that has resulted from your growth in relationship with Him? If not, what does the Holy Spirit want you to do to equip you for these important tasks?

Take the time to hear from the Lord right now. He has been waiting to share His heart with you.

Chapter 3

Honor Your Father and Mother

"You don't love your father."

The Lord's still, small voice spoke clearly in Mark's heart during a worship service. Startled, Mark replied, "I don't hate my father."

The Lord said again, "You don't love your father!"

Again Mark responded, "Well, I don't hate him, either!"

Earlier that year, Mark and his father had had a rather intense disagreement when Mark had tried to teach his father the things he was learning in his spiritual life. His father had been resistant to Mark's input, and relations had been strained ever since. Mark had decided to back off and no longer try to "bring up his parents in the nurture and admonition of the Lord," recognizing that it was out of biblical order. However, the closeness of the relationship had been broken, and neither man had any inclination to make the first move toward restoring it.

Now the Lord was saying, "Mark, you are indifferent. You do not actively love and honor your father, as I have commanded. Love is not static or apathetic. Love is an active verb, and you do not love your father."

Mark recognized the truth of the Lord's words, and repented immediately.

"Honor your father and mother. This is the first of God's Ten Commandments that ends with a promise. And this is the promise: that if you honor your father and mother, yours will be a long life, full of blessing." (Ephesians 6:2,3 TLB)

If you thought this chapter was finally going to get down to the nitty-gritty of what we need to teach our children, I'm sorry but I'll have to disappoint you. I want to talk, not primarily about what your children should do, but rather about what *you* should do. Remember, our goal is to open up the channels of grace to flow into you and your children and your home. Your relationship with your parents will have a great influence on the state of grace in your own home.

Charlie Shedd has stated, "The greatest gift a man can give his children is to love their mother." The parents' attitude and treatment of one another will set the tone for the household. Children will have no more respect for their mother than their father does. They will honor their father no more than their mother does. In addition, children learn how to treat their spouses from the way their parents treat one another, and the tenor of the families of the next generation is thus established.

My mother always told me, "Watch how a man treats his mother, because that is how he will treat his wife. If he doesn't respect his mother, he won't respect you. If he is not understanding with his mother, he will not be understanding with you." In other words, if a man does not honor his father and mother, he will not honor his wife. If he does not honor his wife, neither will his children. (The same holds true for the wife.) All relationships within a family are shaped by the relationships of the couple with their own parents.

What Is "Honor"?

What exactly does it mean to "honor" your parents? Other biblical references indicate that it includes highly prizing (Proverbs 4:8), showing respect for (Leviticus 19:3), and obeying (Deuteronomy 21:18–21). Webster states that it further means to show high regard for them. We often talk about the need for *children* to honor their parents, by which we usually mean they must respect and obey them. But is there reason to assume that in the middle of addressing the Ten Commandments to the adults of the nation of Israel, without any explanation or clarifying remarks, God threw in one command meant only for the children, then immediately

went back to speaking to the adults? Do we have any justifi-
cation for applying this directive only to people under
eighteen years of age?

I don't think so. I believe that, like the rest of the Ten
Commandments, this instruction was for all the children of
Abraham, that is, all believers of every age. So, what would
honoring your parents look like in a thirty or forty-year-old
married individual? At a minimum, it would involve an
attitude of respect when you speak to or about them.

Because they have lived longer than you and experienced
more than you, their wisdom and knowledge are greater than
yours. You should seek out their opinions and advice, and
really take the time to listen to them. Recognize their unique
gifts and talents, and honestly esteem them. Offer your gifts
to them as they need them, and draw upon their gifts to
enhance and enrich your life, as they are willing to give them.

As your parents grow older, you may find your role evolving
toward that of caregiver rather than care-recipient. Recognize
their new needs and weaknesses without allowing your
attitude toward them to deteriorate. Be patient and kind and
understanding, willingly altering your lifestyle as necessary
for the care and comfort of those who have given so much to
you. When the subject of your parents comes up in your
home, let your words reflect your honor and respect for them,
and do not allow any other member of your family to show
disrespect for them.

Those of us with loving parents find this fairly easy to do.
After all, they deserve our honor. But what about those whose
parents were less than loving and accepting, those who were
even violent and cruel? Can their adult children be expected
to respect such unworthy individuals?

There are no exception clauses to God's command, and we
cannot even claim it is Old Covenant and therefore does not
apply to us, since it is repeated in Ephesians. But perhaps the
Lord recognized how difficult it would be for some of us to
honor our sinful parents. Maybe that is why He included a
promise with this command. If we are unable or unwilling to
honor our parents for their sake or even for the Lord's sake,
perhaps we will do it for our own sakes. It is in our own best
interests to give honor to our parents, for then God Himself

will ensure that it will go well with us and we will enjoy a long and happy life on the earth (Ephesians 6:3). You have God's own promise that if you will honor your parents, your life will be blessed.

Two days after Mark's conversation with the Lord referred to at the beginning of this chapter, we received a letter from Mark's father. When we built our first house, we had borrowed money from our parents at a competitive interest rate. Now, Mark's father was writing to say that the Lord had convicted him about charging us, as fellow believers, interest on our loan. He had added up the payments we had made so far and found that they were enough to cover the repayment of the original loan. He was therefore writing to say that he considered our loan paid in full! "Honor your father and mother, that it may go well with thee!" We were so blessed to have such an immediate affirmation of God's promise to us.

Honoring our parents does not only apply to those parents who are still living, either. It is just as important to maintain an attitude of honor and respect toward those who have passed away. Counselees often protest, "I can't forgive my father for abusing me. He has been dead for fifteen years." They must come to understand that forgiveness, honor and respect are not primarily for the benefit of those on the receiving end but for those on the giving end. Unforgiveness, bitterness, dishonor and disrespect become cancers that eat away in the spirit of those who harbor them. Though our deceased relatives are no longer harmed by our bad attitudes, and will not be helped by our changed feelings, we ourselves are being held prisoner by our hostility. Honoring our parents, whether living or dead, will bring release within our own hearts, as well as a release of God's blessings upon us.

The Laws of the Harvest

There are other reasons why we as adults should continue to honor our fathers and mothers.

> *"Do not be deceived: God cannot be mocked. A man reaps what he sows. The one who sows to please his sinful nature, from that nature will reap destruction; the one who sows to*

please the Spirit, from the Spirit will reap eternal life. Let us not become weary in doing good, for at the proper time we will reap a harvest if we do not give up. Therefore, as we have opportunity, let us do good to all people ... "

(Galatians 6:7–10)

It is an unchanging law of the universe that what we sow we will indeed reap. If we sow honor, we will reap honor. If we sow love, we will reap love. If we sow scorn, we will reap scorn. If we sow discord, we will reap discord. If we sow according to our carnal, sinful impulses, we will reap destruction.

Every word, deed and attitude you have toward your own parents is a seed that is planted in the spirit realm. God has promised that you will eat the fruit of every seed you sow. You will receive back, in your children's words, deeds and attitudes toward you, a harvest from your seeds. Are you sowing seeds that will produce the behavior you want your children to express toward you in your later years?

Related to the law of sowing and reaping is the law of increase, which demands that what we reap be greater than what we sow. We do not expect to receive back as a harvest exactly the same amount as we sow, else what is the point of sowing? We sow one kernel of corn and reap hundreds of kernels. We sow one squash seed and reap an abundance of zucchini. We sow to the wind and reap the whirlwind (Hosea 8:7). We sow disrespect for our parents, and we reap rebellion from our children. We sow honor for our parents, and we reap esteem and admiration from our children.

Do not be deceived: God is not mocked. He wants us to honor our parents so much that He has even appealed to our own enlightened self-interest to get us to do it. Though we may grow weary in honoring those who do not seem to deserve it or respond to it, God has promised that He will give us the rewards He has promised: a blessed life and honor from our own children.

The Sins of the Fathers ...

In Chapter 1 we talked about the sins of previous generations being visited upon our children. This concept is related to the law of sowing and reaping, for what one generation sows, future generations will be forced to reap. If you have been disrespectful and lacking in honor toward your parents, your children will reap the consequences of that sin. Through repentance and turning away from your sinful attitudes, and drawing upon the grace of God to replace them with His Spirit of love, you can unstop this channel of grace, allowing the promised blessing of a long, full life to flow freely into your children's lives.

Teach Honor by Honoring

Finally, you are mentoring your children by your relationship with your parents. You are teaching them by example how children are to treat parents. If your children hear you mocking your father's forgetfulness, they will learn that it is acceptable for children to ridicule their parents. If your children hear you complaining about the time you must spend listening to your mother's litany of physical aches and pains, they will learn that the needs of others are unimportant. If your children see you seek out the opinion of your father on how to remodel the basement, they will learn that it is not a sign of weakness to receive input from their elders. If your children hear you praising your mother's famous dessert, they will learn that it is good to give honor where honor is due.

Do you want your children to honor you? Honor *your* father and mother!

Time to Hear from God

Think for a moment about your attitude toward your parents. Do you actively honor them or their memory? Do you honestly love and respect them? Do you seek out their wisdom and insight for decisions you have to make? Do you listen to their stories with interest and attention? Do you try to meet their needs while guarding their dignity and self-respect? Do you talk to your children about them with words and spirit that express honor and esteem?

Do you complain about time you must spend meeting their needs? Do you belittle their weaknesses? Are you angry and resentful about the way they treated you when you were a child? Are you harboring bitterness against them for not protecting you from harm, as you trusted them to protect you? Do you use expressions of dishonor when referring to them ("the old man" or "my old lady")? Do you allow your children to speak disrespectfully to or about them?

How often are you in contact with them? Do you call, write or visit regularly? Do you know what is going on in their lives? Do you know about their health concerns and what their latest doctor's visit revealed?

Take some time right now to quiet yourself in the Lord's presence and ask Him to show you clearly your attitude toward your father and mother. Come with a humble spirit, willing to hear the truth. If He points out any ways in which you have been unforgiving or disrespectful, if you have been anything less than honoring in your attitude toward your parents, wholeheartedly repent and ask for God's grace to cleanse your heart and purify your spirit. Ask Him what fruits of repentance He wants you to produce, then draw upon His grace to do as He directs.

Chapter 4

The Golden Rule

Karen and Margo were standing in the back of the church after service one Sunday. It had been a long time since they had seen each other and they had a lot of catching up to do. Around them, the crowd mingled, moving toward the door with friendly greetings. Every once in a while, Margo or Karen would respond to a friend's cheery, "So long!" but their conversation continued despite the frequent interruptions. In fact, they hardly even noticed them.

Then Alice walked up to Karen and gave her a big hug. Smiling an apology to Margo, Karen returned the hug and greeted Alice. Quickly she was incorporated into the conversation, with no apparent break. "You weren't at the ladies' meeting on Thursday, Karen, and the little favors were so adorable, I wanted to make sure you got one. Here it is – I saved it just for you."

Suitable admiration and exclamations were made over Alice's gift, and she moved on to another group. Karen and Margo continued their chat. Suddenly Johnny, Karen's four-year-old son, cannoned into her legs. "Mommy! Look what I made for you in Sunday School! Look, Mommy! See? Isn't it pretty? Don't you like it? Look, Mommy! I made it just for you! Look, Mommy!" With each "Look, Mommy!" the volume and intensity increased.

At first, Karen continued her conversation with Margo, seemingly oblivious to the little whirlwind that had descended upon them. Margo, however, being a dedicated career woman

61

with no children of her own, was increasingly distracted by the noise and activity. Finally, when Johnny's volume reached such heights that people around were beginning to stare and she could no longer hear Margo's questions, Karen reached down, put a hand over Johnny's mouth and said sharply, "Can't you see I am talking to someone? Don't interrupt!" With no hesitation, she turned back to Margo and, in a sweet voice asked, "What was that you just said?"

After further futile attempts to attract and hold his mother's attention, Johnny dropped his gift and wandered outside to play on the swings with the other children. Five minutes later, Karen and Margo said their good-byes and Karen began looking around for Johnny. Seeing him across the yard, she called out, "Johnny! Time to go home! Come on now, Johnny! It's time to leave!" But Johnny just kept right on playing without seeming to even hear his mother. Somewhat embarrassed, Karen ruefully said to the pastor's wife, "That boy! It's like he doesn't even hear my voice! I think I'm going to have to borrow that book on the strong-willed child from the church library. I just don't know what is wrong with him!"

"Therefore, whatever you want men to do to you, do also to them ..."   (Matthew 7:12 NKJV)

"However you want people to treat you, so treat them ..."
(Matthew 7:12 NAS)

"In everything, therefore, treat people the same way you want them to treat you, for this is the Law and the Prophets."
(Matthew 7:12 NASU)

As a guiding principle for all of life, it would be hard to improve on the Golden Rule. It is so simple, so obvious, so absolutely right. It doesn't need explanations or detailed analysis. It doesn't require an in-depth knowledge of the Greek or an advanced degree in theology to comprehend and apply. Even a child can understand what is required by this simple command, yet Jesus declares that it is the summary of all of the teachings of the Law and the Prophets. No other law would be necessary if only God's people would follow this one! How amazing! How incredible!

Skeptics have tried to devalue the force of the Golden Rule and the incredible wisdom it represents by saying that it was not new with Jesus. Confucius and other ancient teachers had long promoted the so-called "Silver Rule:" "Don't do to anyone else what you wouldn't want done to you." Jesus put His own little twist on the words, but essentially they were just borrowed from other ancient wise men, they assert.

Such claims fail to recognize the vast difference between these two exhortations. The Silver Rule is not bad, but it is essentially a passive ordinance. If you don't want people to hit you, don't hit them. If you don't want to be gossiped about, don't gossip about others. If you don't want to be prejudged, don't be prejudiced against others. In the context of the law of sowing and reaping, it basically says, "If you don't want to eat broccoli, don't plant it!"

The Golden Rule, on the other hand, is an active decree. If you want to be respected, respect others. If you want to be loved, love others. If you want to be welcomed into others' homes, be hospitable. If you want to be judged with mercy, judge others with mercy. If you want others to listen to you, listen to others.

However you feel you deserve to be treated by strangers, treat strangers that way. However you want to be treated by your friends, treat your friends that way. *And however you want your children to treat you, treat them!* How obvious, right? Yet how often do we ignore or neglect these basic teachings of our faith, pursuing instead some "deeper truth."

I never cease to be amazed at the way people, even Christians, treat children. For some reason we have embraced the world's view that children are somehow less important, less worthy, less *human* than adults, and therefore the normal rules of propriety and etiquette need not be applied in dealing with them. It is apparently completely appropriate to ignore, belittle, mock, criticize, embarrass, and even humiliate children. Their needs, interests and desires are of secondary importance, merely because of their age. They are often expected to act like miniature adults without being accorded the simple dignity of a person of value.

What is the logical, biblical or reasonable foundation for the belief that "Children are to be seen and not heard"? Have you embraced this philosophy? If so, why? Are you simply copying the way your parents raised you, without thinking for yourself or seeking the mind of the Lord for your own life? Can you biblically justify your philosophy on the place of children in the home, the Church and society?

It was exciting to me when I was writing this chapter to discover the context of the Golden Rule: Jesus was talking about the relationship between parents and children!

> *"Or what man is there among you, when his son shall ask him for a loaf, will give him a stone? Or if he shall ask for a fish, he will not give him a snake, will he? If you then, being evil, know how to give good gifts to your children, how much more shall your Father who is in heaven give what is good to those who ask Him!* **Therefore**, *however you want people* [i.e., any human being] *to treat you, so treat them, for this is the Law and the Prophets."* (Matthew 7:9–12)

It is not stretching the meaning of this verse at all to apply it to your actions and attitudes toward your children. Clearly, you are to say or do nothing to your children that you would not want said or done to you, and you are to speak and act toward your children the way you want them to speak and act toward you!

And beyond that, it is also clear from the context that the way you treat your children will influence the way they see God. Your child's subconscious picture of God will be based on the way you treat him. He will expect to be treated by God the way he has been treated by his parents. He will define his relationship with God by his relationship with you. What picture of God are you giving your children?

However You Want People to Treat You ...

There are at least four reasons to make the Golden Rule your guiding principle:

1. It establishes a standard by which you can always and instantly judge your actions. How would you want to be treated in this situation? That is how you will treat everyone else. It is a standard for your behavior that is set by the Lord Jesus Christ. It is the right way for a child of God to act.

2. It is closely related to the Law of the Harvest, or the Law of Sowing and Reaping. Although it is not stated in this way, it is implied that the way you treat others is the way you will be treated. The actions you sow will come back to you in the conduct of others toward you. By obeying the Golden Rule, you will be sowing the kind of behavior into your children's lives that you want to reap from them.

3. It is a way of training by modeling. By being a living demonstration of holiness, kindness, forgiveness, forbearance, mercy, and love, you are an example that they may follow as you follow Christ.

4. It gives you the opportunity to be an expression of the holiness and love of God in your home, planting within your children a positive revelation of His goodness toward them.

Let's get specific. What actions and attitudes do I want my children to express?

I want my children to be considerate of my feelings and the feelings of others. I will therefore be mindful of their feelings, not deliberately placing them in positions where they will be embarrassed, not demeaning them either publicly or privately, not making light of the pressures and problems they face.

Instead, I will invite them to be honest about their feelings, and receive them without judgment. I will not "freak out," no matter what they have to tell me. I will listen to them with my physical ears while listening to the Holy Spirit with my spiritual ears. I will try to see circumstances from their perspective, and teach them to do the same for others.

I will help them recognize the source of negative emotions and teach them how to draw upon the grace of God to overcome them. I will rejoice with them when they rejoice, not belittling their victories but celebrating them whole-heartedly. I will weep with them when they weep, not scorning their sorrows but sharing them. I will accept that if they weep, it is because they *have* something to cry about, whether I would cry about it or not. If they are wounded, they have the right to cry, and I will be there to comfort and support them as I want to be comforted and supported when I hurt. I will not lecture or deride, but, like the great Comforter, I will come alongside to help.

I want my children to respect me. Therefore, I will respect them as special, unique creations of God placed in my care for a very short time. When they speak, I will listen. I will seek out their opinions on all sorts of subjects. We will learn to disagree agreeably, with respect and honor for each other as individuals of value, not allowing issues to cloud the impor-tance of people and relationships. I will at all times speak to them in a pleasant and respectful tone of voice. I will not allow my emotions (no matter how justified!) to become more important to me than the dignity and feelings of my children. I will trust them to be well-behaved, kind, courteous and compassionate. (Respect is so important that we will focus the entire next chapter on it.)

I want my children to respect my privacy. I will therefore respect their right to privacy. I will invite their confidences, but not demand them as my right. Because I understand the need everyone has for personal space, their bedroom shall be their haven, and I will not demand control over it or access to it. I will respect a closed door, not opening it without permission. The record of their conversations with God (their journals) will be for their eyes only, and I will not intrude upon this relationship without invitation.

I want my children to show compassion for those weaker than themselves, so I will be compassionate of their weaknesses. Whether physical, emotional, social, academic, or spiritual, I will never make light of my children's weakness or use it against them. Instead, I will quietly offer myself and my gifts to take hold along with them in their areas of weakness. I will help them discover and develop their own gifts, so they may grow in self-confidence and healthy personal pride. I will recognize that each of us has our own weak spots, and that is part of what makes us unique. I will therefore neither look up in adulation nor down in scorn on any other creation of God.

I want my children to listen when I speak to them. Therefore, I will listen when they speak to me. I will recognize the honor that they do me by inviting me to be a part of their world, and I will receive that honor with gratitude. When they are young, I will teach them how to get my attention politely, and when they do, I will reward them with my interest. However, I will recognize that young children have an inaccurate concept of time, so their ability to wait for my attention is very limited. Therefore, I will meet their needs as quickly as politely possible.

This may be a good time to address the situation with little Johnny, from the story at the beginning of this chapter. I suppose the typical Christian reaction would be that he needed to learn not to interrupt when adults were talking. Personally, I have a problem with that. Adults interrupt each other all the time; they have just learned to do it more politely. Therefore, I believe that Karen should have taken the opportunity to teach Johnny good manners.

In a similar situation, if I were Karen, I would immediately place my hand on Johnny's head as soon as he arrived by my side so that he knew I had acknowledged his presence. Then, as soon as possible, I would say to Margo, "Excuse me just a moment, would you please?" Then I would give Johnny my complete attention while he showed me his creation, give him a quick hug, then say, "But did you notice that Mommy was talking to someone else? You should always say, 'Excuse me' when you must interrupt another conversation, okay? Can you say 'Excuse me' to Miss Margo now? Good boy! Now, why don't I hold my present while you go outside and play for just a few more minutes?"

This would have made the interruption no more intrusive or impolite than Alice's was, but would have honored the dignity of Johnny's personhood and his gift, and provided an opportunity for lifestyle instruction.

Beyond listening to the words my children say, I want to listen to their hearts. I want to be as aware of what they are *not* saying as I am of what they *are* saying. I want to hear not just the words but also the real meaning behind them. When they say, "I won't!" I want to discern if it is rebellion or fear or embarrassment or hurt or sickness that is motivating them. I will learn how to ask probing questions with a gentle spirit, so my children will know they are safe in trusting their hearts to me.

I want my children to voluntarily help others, so I will freely offer my help to them. I will be careful to come alongside to help them, sharing the load with them without taking it from them so they will not feel inadequate or unnecessary. Even their assigned household chores will sometimes be a group effort so we can all share the joy of cooperative labor. We will also give our help to others outside our home, as a family sharing with other parts of God's family.

I want my children to be grateful, so I will cultivate an attitude of gratitude within myself. I will frequently and deliberately express my gratitude to the Lord for all He is and all He does. "His praise shall continually be in my mouth." In addition, I will express my appreciation to all those around me who make my life easier and better. I will thank the waitress and cashier, the deliveryman and the gas station attendant. Because they do their jobs well, I am blessed. Therefore, I will bless them in return.

I will especially make it a point to say "Thank you" to members of my family. The little kindnesses and considerations that family members do for one another on a daily basis are the oil that lubricate against the natural friction that may occur among any group of unique individuals. Letting each other know that you have recognized their efforts and appreciate them makes us all more willing to continue to be thoughtful.

Mark has always been vocally appreciative of whatever I do for him, and he always compliments me and thanks me for every meal I prepare for him. Without any instruction or encouragement from us, Chari and Josh began to follow his example. Now it has become a friendly contest to see who can be the first to say, "Great meal, Mom (or Patti)! Thanks!" They not only say it to me; they are quick to express their thanks whenever we eat out as well. And if we have eaten at a restaurant, Mark receives everyone's gratitude for a great meal.

Have you ever received a gift that wasn't exactly what you wanted? In fact, it was about as far from your tastes as one can get? How did you respond? Did you become offended because the person who supposedly loved you didn't know you well enough to know you would hate it? Or did you look into their heart to see their desire to please, even if they had failed? Were you grateful for their love? Were you able to cherish the gift because of who gave it, even if not for itself?

We were at a friend's home shortly after Christmas, and my heart was fairly broken by the way they talked about the gifts they had received. Keep in mind, this was a strong Christian family, leaders in their local church. The mother, Terry, had arranged for satellite television hook-up as her gift to her husband, Frank. She knew how much he enjoyed watching sports and thought he would be excited about the great variety that would now be available to him. Instead, he spent the next week complaining about what a waste of money it was. Not only would they be paying out every month for this stupid thing, but there would be the ugly satellite dish messing up the property. I did not hear one word of gratitude or pleasure at the thoughtfulness of his wife the whole time we were there.

Their daughter Chris happened to be going through a Barbie-doll stage at the time, so Terry had bought some fabric and patterns for outfits that she and Chris could sew together, as well as a Barbie vehicle. "Why didn't you just buy the dresses? I can't make these! They're too little. And that's not the car I wanted. I *told* you I wanted the jeep. Why did you get this? It's so stupid. I didn't want this." Chris' whining continued throughout the week. Not a thank you. Not any expression of pleasure. Only rejection and complaints. I wonder where she learned to act like that?

I want my children to be polite to me and everyone else. I will therefore take care to always use good manners in my home. I am continually amazed at the lack of courtesy and downright rudeness I hear in Christian households. I cannot understand why one would carefully use his best manners in conversation with a stranger whom he may never see again, while completely ignoring them in conversations with the most important people in his life. If you absolutely must be rude to someone, at least make it to someone who is not dear to you!

Mark has always been what is now considered old-fashioned about the roles of men and women. I, personally, consider him courteous and even chivalrous. He never allows a woman to carry anything heavy if he is around, and believes it is the job of the man to protect and care for the woman. Not being a women's lib proponent, I really appreciate his attitude.

Another of his habits is to always open the door for me, and he even gets offended if I don't wait for him to do so. He has always opened the car door for me, even at home where no one else sees. No one, that is, except for our children. Sometime in his teen years, without anyone telling him he should or asking him to do so, Joshua started opening the car door for Charity while Mark is opening my door. Charity is the one who usually drives when we are all together, and it still gives me pleasure to see Josh walk around the car to let her in before climbing in the back himself.

When they see courtesy and good manners demonstrated on a daily basis in their home, our children learn to act that way themselves. They don't need constant reminders to be polite in public, because they will have developed those habits at home. Anything less than the civility they are used to will be looked at with distaste, and they will have no desire to lower themselves to such behavior.

Why is it considered appropriate to give orders to children, rather than phrasing our instructions as a request? What is wrong with saying, "Would you please close the door?" rather than, "Shut the door!"? What is wrong with saying, "Thank you" when they do what is expected of them? Jesus says that it is servants who do not expect consideration or gratitude for doing their jobs. Are our children no more than servants in our homes? Is this the way the Lord intends it to be?

In what other contexts are people required to simply take orders without expecting them to be expressed courteously? Some people in management positions like to tell their subordinates what to do without politeness or civility. Barking out orders and watching their "inferiors" scurry to do their bidding seems to give them a feeling of power and superiority that their weak egos need. These individuals certainly have no respect for those under their command, and studies have proven that they do not stimulate the same level of loyalty or productivity that more secure, and therefore courteous, leaders inspire.

In the military one is also expected to take orders without question. The drill sergeant bellowing out his commands shows no respect for his underlings because he *can* have no thought for them as individuals. They must become a unit, a cohesive fighting machine that responds instantly to whatever orders they receive. Their effectiveness in carrying out their mission as well as their own personal safety may depend upon their subordination of their own will and immediate obedience to their commander.

Is that what we want from our children? More importantly, is that what God wants from our children? Is that the most effective way to prepare them for the destiny for which they were created?

We often use the excuse that we can't help becoming angry with our children, that they drive us crazy, and that we sometimes just lose control. That is why we scream and yell and screech at them – we just can't help it! Perhaps. But what would happen if, in the middle of your "uncontrollable" tirade, the telephone rang? What tone of voice would you use to answer it? Or suppose your pastor suddenly rang the doorbell? Are you really as "out of control" as you would like to think you are? Or would you be fully able to speak in a pleasant tone to someone who was "important"?

We have some lovely Christian friends who are warm, generous people generally doing a good job of raising their children. But I am always surprised while talking on the phone with them. She may be sharing about the great church service on Sunday and how awesome the worship was, when suddenly her voice changes and she yells, *"Andy, leave your sister alone!"* Then, she instantly switches back to her normal tone and continues talking to me, "And there was such an anointing on the pastor. The Word came forth with such

power ... *Sally, put that down right now* ... and the ministry
time was so wonderful ... *Sally, I'm not going to tell you again!"*

We are good friends, but I honestly don't think I am more
important to her than her children are. I know she loves them
dearly and wants to be the best mother possible. So why does
she speak politely to me and shrilly to them? I truly don't
believe it is deliberate. I think it is just a habit that she
developed and has never really thought about.

One of our neighbors had a little girl just a few months after
Charity was born, so we often shared our concerns as first-
time moms. When Hillary was about 18 months old, Catherine became bothered by how much of Hillary's talking was
actually whining. She didn't just ask her mother for a cookie
in a normal tone. It was always in that nasal, whining voice
that is designed to drive mothers crazy.

Catherine was a strong disciplinarian type parent, so she did
her best to break Hillary of what was fast becoming a habit.
Then, one day the Lord opened Catherine's ears to the sound
of her own voice when she was changing Hillary's diaper and
cleaning up after her meal. She was amazed to hear the same
whiny quality coming out of her mouth that she so disliked in
her daughter! Because her heart was soft toward God, she
immediately repented and began trying to remove the log
from her own eye before dealing any more with the speck in
Hillary's.

Maybe it is time for us all to think about the tone of voice
we use with our children. Is it a voice we want to hear them
using toward each other? Is it a tone we want them to take
with us? Is it really the tone that God wants us to be using
with anyone, especially those whom He has given us the
responsibility to disciple?

These are just some of the ways in which the Golden Rule
applies to raising children. If we as adults will live our faith in
our most important relationships – with our spouse, our
children and our parents – many of our problems and
questions will fall by the wayside.

It's Your Turn

Now it is time for you to ask the Holy Spirit how He wants you to apply the Golden Rule in your home. What attitudes and behaviors does He want to instill in your children? What can you do to be used by Him to draw them forth? As the Lord guides you, make a list of your priorities (or, more appropriately, God's priorities for you) and your part in treating your children the way you want them to treat you and others.

Chapter 5

Respect Everyone
In Every Way

"I learned almost a year in advance that we would be having very distinguished visitors coming to stay with us. No one seemed to know for how long, except to say that we should prepare for a long visit, as they were being sent to learn absolutely everything they could about their host community and country, and they come with very little preparation.

People who had recently had similar visitors said we should treat them as if they were truly honored guests, even though no one seems to know exactly from whence they came. Everyone agrees they didn't speak the same language and knew almost nothing about our culture, but they were very malleable and flexible, often, but not always, easy to get along with (in fact, they can be very demanding, I was told), and, above all, very fast learners. So fast, in fact, we would often have to struggle to keep up.

And so we prepared our house for the arrival of our distinguished visitors as best we knew how. We wanted them to feel comfortable, safe, and secure, as if this were their own home. And once we readied the space, we began to think about what we would want their sojourn to be like.

We'll want them to explore. We'll try to introduce them to the best that we have to offer – the wonders of our natural environment and a community that will welcome them with open arms. We will share with them what we think to be important – our religion, our culture, our music, our creative arts – but we'll make sure to introduce them to the religions, arts, and culture of our neighbors, too. We might even get to take them to all those places in our community and maybe even the whole country that we'd always wanted to visit, but have put off in the crush of our day-to-day lives.

We'll help them with languages – our forms of reading and writing, our sometimes strange ways of doing mathematics, our language of music so they can open doors to our houses of wisdom and so they can learn about who we really are. We'll make a special effort to introduce them to people different from ourselves, so they could experience the rich kaleidoscope that makes where we are a great place to live.

We'll feed them nourishing food. Not fancy every night – that's not the way we eat – but simple, nutritious fare, though we'd make sure they'd get to experience our festive foods as well. We expect they'll like some of it, and probably some items they'll move to the edge of the plate, at least for a time until they get used to them. And maybe, for some of our foods, they may never develop a taste. Palates differ, and we'll respect that.

We'll learn to respect their needs for privacy, for time alone and in nature, and give them enough space to express and pursue their own interests and desires. These may differ from our own, and indeed it would be surprising if they didn't, given that they come from another place and another time. They may even develop their own tastes in clothing and hairstyles, and their own musical subculture, blending what we have to offer with their own native sense of style.

We'll try to alert them to dangers they might encounter. I do not know if they are aware of our traffic habits, or the swift-moving tide in the inlet, our addictions, or even how our gas stove works. They'll get comfortable soon enough, but as the maxim reads, 'Safety First.'

They might want to spend time with other visitors in our community, maybe just to compare notes and share common thoughts and feelings. We'll try to make sure they have opportunities to do so, though we'll be sure to check in with the other hosts first. We've also been told that our visitors may like to try out our sports with each other, and if we choose, they might even allow us to join in.

Of course, they'll have to learn something about our community's rules. We've developed them over time, and they have stood us in pretty good stead, though sometimes even we forget why they are there. Having to keep our visitors informed will be a good reminder. And since they will be living under the same rules as we do, as soon as they are fully familiar with our rules and traditions, we'll invite them to join us in improving upon them.

We'll expect that they will change over time. Whenever I've spent time in a foreign land, even for short periods, I've come back a changed person. How much more would I have been transformed if my sojourn had been a prolonged one!

We'll try to learn to relax around them. I expect this will be difficult for a while, but we'll learn, too – I'm sure we'll have as much to learn from them as they do from us.

I guess I'm not too concerned about how many facts or concepts that we've developed they take away with them. If these enrich their visit and help them in the future, so much the better. But what I really hope they'll take away is the knowledge that our community and our nation, and with them our individual and collective happiness, is built upon the responsible exercise of freedom. It's a freedom they were born with, and I hope they will be able to take along with them, unfettered by prejudice, their own or that of others, unhampered to the highest degree possible by others' expectations, or their own preconceptions, fears, and self-doubts, uninhibited by dependencies not freely chosen.

I know that I will grow to love my visitors, and expect that they will grow to love me. We will have shared so much together! Someday, of course, and I hope not too soon, they'll leave and continue on their respective journeys. I hope they'll continue to write, and call, and maybe we'll even be able to get together from time to time. I hope they'll someday look back at our time together and, faced with the prospect of distinguished visitors themselves, be able to say, and really mean it, 'That's where I learned how to treat an honored guest.'"[1]

In the last chapter we touched briefly on the concept of showing respect to our children. What do I mean by respecting children? Am I one of those humanists who espouse children's rights to an equal voice in the household? Do I believe that children are born inherently good and it is only their exposure to the evils of the world that contaminates them?

No, absolutely not. David declared, *"In sin did my mother conceive me"* (Psalm 51:5). The Bible is clear to state that all the descendants of Adam carry his sinful nature. But, all descendants of Adam also carry the image of God in which he was created, and therefore they are worthy of respect. Webster states that to respect means "to show honor and esteem; to show consideration for." This doesn't mean that children are given equal power with you; it just means that they are valued. Children are a heritage, an inheritance, a reward given to you by the Lord (Psalm 127:3ff.). They are creations of His Holy Spirit entrusted into your care. Would you insult your Lord by treating the precious gifts He has given to you disrespectfully?

In many places and times of human history, children have been primarily viewed as cheap labor. When the bare sustenance of life is dependent on the daily efforts of the family, an extra pair of hands could be the difference between survival and starvation. Any one individual's inherent value as a creation and child of God is irrelevant. Children are mere commodities of production. Christianity does not take that view. Just as the Scriptures have raised the position of women from inferior beings to co-inheritors of the Kingdom of God, so also have they raised children from mere slaves to co-heirs.

First Peter 2:17 calls us to a very high standard: *"Honor all* [men] ... *"* The word for "honor" means "to revere, to prize, to value, and to respect." The word "men" is not found in the original Greek; Peter merely said to honor *all*, meaning we are to respect and value "all, any, every, anyone, everyone, in every way, thoroughly."[2] It would appear that Peter was including children in this exhortation: we are even to honor children.

We have already talked about some ways you can show your respect for your children. You can allow and even encourage them to make decisions from an early age. If they have accepted Jesus as their Lord and Savior, know how to recognize His voice within them, and are walking in obedience and submission to Him, you can express your respect for this by trusting their ability and willingness to hear from God. When they must make a decision, talk about the consequences of all possibilities, encourage them to journal about it (write out their conversation with God), submit it to you if necessary, and then accept the consequences.

Another expression of respect is to answer when your children call and listen when they speak. Is there anyone else in the world we would ignore as rudely as we do our children? Why do we do this? What possible scriptural support can we find for a view that children are less worthy of courtesy and respect than adults?

It is also important to answer your children's questions when they are asked. If they want to know what a word means, give them a coherent accurate definition. If you can't do that off the top of your head, look it up together in a dictionary. If they want to know how something works, explain it to the best of your ability. If you don't know, try to find someone who does know or go to the library and look it up together. Purchase a good quality up-to-date encyclopedia set or learn how to use those available online.

Not only is this an expression of respect, it is also the most valuable and effective education you can give your children. We all learn best when the information is relevant to us and we really want to learn it. When your children ask a question, they are indicating what they are ready to learn. Make the most of this opportunity. Vocabulary lessons aren't boring when they grow out of what the child is currently interested in. Just be sure that you are accurate! I have been amazed many times when my off-the-cuff definitions have come back to me word-for-word from the mouths of my kids. If you don't know for sure, don't be embarrassed to say so and search out the answers together. Your eagerness to learn new things will stimulate a similar willingness in your children. Chari and Josh still enjoy learning new words and often use their exercise times to increase their verbal as well as physical strength.

Does Self-Expression = Rebellion?

An area we as adults, and perhaps especially as Christians, struggle with respecting is our children's right to self-expression. Part of the maturing process is self-individuation – discovering and expressing the uniqueness of who God made us. Some of these expressions are predictable and group-oriented, as each generation develops its own style of music, dress, and slang. Others are more specific demonstrations of our child's individual gifts and interests. Some are simply ways of moving out of their position as "child," and others are acts of rebellion. Certainly we need the wisdom and grace of God to know how to respond properly to whatever our children do!

We have a friend who named her son James, after her husband. Because the father was called Jim, the son was nicknamed Jamie. However, when he was thirteen years old, Jamie decided that "Jamie" was a sissy name and he wanted to be called James. To me, that seemed a realistic request. After all, Jamie (James!) had had no voice in what he was named and nicknamed originally, so if he was uncomfortable with it, if it was making his teen life more difficult, why shouldn't he be called James? It was, after all, his legal name. It wasn't as if he wanted to change it to Mephistopheles, for goodness sake!

When our son Joshua was young, we tended to call him "Joshy." There came a day when he asked us to use either Joshua or Josh, and we all made the effort to fulfill his request. Well, our friend didn't see it that way. "He's my son and I named him Jamie and if I want to call him Jamie, I will!" she declared. And she steadfastly refused to even try to remember to call him James. Unfortunately, that was only one symptom of the problems that existed in their relationship, and her insensitivity to his needs only served to alienate him further.

Our children went through times of experimenting with their unique self-expression. When Charity was fourteen years old, she began toying with the ideas of either getting a tattoo or having a colored streak put in her hair. Because a tattoo is permanent but hair grows out, we encouraged her to hold off on the tattoo until she was old enough to be sure she would really want to have it the rest of her life. However, when she was sure about what she wanted done with her hair, she had our permission.

She saw a woman with a white streak on one side of her head and thought that was the look she wanted, so our hairdresser bleached out a section on the front of her right side. I have to say that all of our conservative homeschooling friends were quite shocked when they saw her! She was the oldest homeschooler in our support group and had been somewhat of a pioneer before the younger ones. However, the streak really looked very attractive and accomplished what she wanted – it set her apart as a unique individual with somewhat radical tendencies who liked to have people give her a second look! Eventually her hair grew out and she let it, not bothering to renew the bleach.

Joshua has also experimented to establish his own look. I remember going to one meeting with him wearing a floor-length coat, sunglasses and a baseball cap on backwards. It doesn't sound so bad when I just say that, but he definitely had a sinister look. I noticed some of the people there giving him sideways glances, trying to figure out who this stranger was. He certainly didn't resemble my Joshua at all. But eventually both Charity and Joshua settled into a modest, attractive look that brings glory to their Lord without compromising their own individuality.

(And incidentally, I learned an important lesson about judging people, especially teenagers, by the way they look. No matter how my kids looked on the outside, they were still good-natured, pure, spiritual individuals on the inside.)

Certainly we must step in if our children want to express themselves in ways that are inconsistent with the Scriptures or dangerous to their health. But I think we tend to step in too soon and too often. If no one will be hurt by their desires, why stop them? Usually once they have experienced what they think they want for a short time, they will return to a more "normal" lifestyle. Don't make any decisions based only on your own feelings. Always seek the mind of the Lord, especially in matters dealing with your children. You need His wisdom.

Give 'em a Break!

You have taught your kids from the beginning to hang up their wet towels after their bath, and they learned the lesson well. None of you have thought about it for months, or even years. It has become a habit that they do without thinking about it. But one morning you walk into their bathroom to find a damp towel lying on the floor, already starting to smell like mildew in the hot summer air. How do you respond?

Do you go charging into your son's bedroom, waving the towel about and screeching about his lack of responsibility? "How many times do I have to tell you to hang up your towel? Why don't you listen when I talk to you? Do you think I have nothing better to do than follow you around all day, picking up after you? Why don't you ever try to help out around here? All I ask is a little consideration! Is that too much to ask? What's the matter with you?" And on and on the lecture goes.

Or do you remember that your son pitched an important play-off game last night and his throwing error allowed the opposing team to score the winning run? He came home exhausted, discouraged, and full of self-doubt. His mind was confused and his thoughts muddled. He didn't leave his towel on the floor out of rebellion or selfishness. He simply forgot, for the first time in eight months. Would it really hurt you to cover his weakness, just this once (1 Peter 4:8)? If it becomes a pattern, then you will have to mention it, but in love and gentleness and with understanding, not anger, wrath and bitterness.

Your daughter reaches across the dinner table for more bread, knocks her glass with her elbow, and for the third time this week, the table is baptized in milk. How do you react? "You clumsy oaf! Would you just slow down and be more careful? Look at this mess! Can't we have just one meal without having to clean up one of your messes?"

But hold on a minute. Did she tip over her milk on purpose? Was it a deliberate act of anger designed to sabotage your lovely meal? Or was it just childishness? Was it just an accident? Have you never spilled anything in your life? How did you feel when you did? Were you embarrassed? Frustrated? Angry with yourself and everyone who witnessed your clumsiness? How did you want the people who saw *your* human frailty to react? Can you respond to your child the way you would want others to respond to you? Can you be patient, loving and kind? Can you ask your child to help you clean up the mess without anger, mockery or fuss?

How do you respond when your child drops your favorite serving bowl while trying to help you dry dishes, or when he wets the bed night after night, or when she has a fender-bender soon after earning her license? These are *accidents*, and by definition, an accident is unintentional! There is no rebellion or sin involved here. And, I dare say, you have had your share of accidents in your life. Like you, your children are aware that they "blew it." They know what they did and the effect it has on other people. They no doubt feel terrible about it already, without your saying a word, just as you would.

However you want people to treat you when you have an accident is your guide to the way you should respond to your children (and spouse) when they have an accident. There is no need to place blame or launch into a long lecture or burst forth in an angry tirade. There is no need to tell anyone else about this embarrassing moment in your child's life. Love covers all sins, wrongs and transgressions (Proverbs 10:12). Do you love your child enough to minimize the fuss and protect his dignity? Do you respect your child enough to accept her as a fallible human being who, like yourself, will make mistakes and have accidents from time to time?

I have noticed that when I am embarrassed, I express it as anger, usually at the situation or inanimate object that "caused" my embarrassment, but sometimes at anyone un-fortunate enough to witness my discomfiture. What do you do if your children express anger when they have been caught in an uncomfortable situation? Do you assume that the anger is an expression of rebellion, which was the actual source of the so-called accident? Or do you recognize it as a defense mechanism thrown up to protect them from further humiliation?

When I am angry because I am embarrassed, I hope that people will say something noncommittal like, "Don't worry about it. It could happen to anyone," or "No big deal. Forget it," then change the subject. That's what I try to do for the people I care about. As a result, embarrassing moments can be quickly forgotten or transformed into amusing anecdotes, rather than exploding into traumatic scenes that leave scars on all involved.

The Ten-year Rule

Long ago I heard two principles that describe my approach to life:

1. Don't sweat the small stuff, and
2. It's all small stuff.

Really, how much of our emotional energy is expended in what is merely "much ado about nothing"? How often do we make our homes into battlefields, arguing and fussing about things that really don't matter in the overall scheme of life? Like Martha, we become worried and bothered about so many things, but only one thing is necessary, only one thing is vitally important, only one thing really matters (Luke 10:41, 42). We must learn to let go of anything that does not affect our relationship with Jesus. We must allow Jesus to show us what is just "small stuff."

Of course it is frustrating when little Johnny tears the knee of his best Sunday outfit. But ten years from now, will it really be important? Was he doing something rebellious or disobedient at the time, or was he just being a little boy? Will that tear in his knee affect his relationship with his Lord? If not, don't overreact. What is more important: your relationship with your child or how the folks at church will look at you if Johnny has a patch on his pants? In the overall scheme of life, what will have more lasting effect on the character of your child: the tear in the pants or the way you respond to it?

Of course it is frustrating when Sally brings home the car with the gas tank empty. But ten years from now, will it really be important? Was it done out of rebellion or deliberate disobedience, or was she just being a teenager, preoccupied with her own affairs? Will that empty gas tank affect her relationship with her Lord? If not, don't overreact. What is more important: your relationship with your nearly-grown child or the fact that you must leave five minutes earlier for church on Sunday? In the overall scheme of life, what will have more lasting effect on the character of your child: the empty gas tank or the way you respond to it?

The "ten-year rule" has often helped me to regain my perspective amid the bedlam that is family life. Ten years from now, will it matter that Tommy wouldn't eat any vegetables? Yes, it will. It will have a definite negative impact on his health as he grows older. But, will it matter that he wouldn't eat any peas? No, there are other vegetables with similar nutritional value he can eat. His tastes do not have to be the same as mine. Which would be more trouble: to steam two vegetables for dinner or to turn the meal into a battle of wills over the peas? Which will leave a more positive deposit in the life and character of your family ten years from now: the nightly battle over who eats what or the example of loving consideration for another's preferences?

The ten-year rule can also help you evaluate your priorities when scheduling conflicts occur. You are supposed to play in a big game for your church baseball league (short stop is a very important position!) on the same night as your daughter's end-of-the-year dance recital (which you really didn't want to go to anyway!). But, ten years from now, who will remember where you were that evening? Whose spirit will still reflect the effects of your decision ten years from now – your team-mates', or your little girl's?

Meet Their Needs

Another important aspect of respecting our children is meeting their needs. Of course, if it is within our power, none of us would ever allow our children to go hungry or cold or without shelter. But there are other needs that children have which, if not met, can leave scars that are just as lasting and destructive.

The senior pastor of a church in which we worked many years ago had recently had another child. One day when we were visiting, the baby was sleeping in a bassinet across the room. Eventually she woke up and began to express her dissatisfaction with being alone and wet and hungry. I had no children yet, but my instinct was to run right over and pick her up. Her mother was of an older, sturdier generation, however. She believed that it was important for a child to cry for a while every day – it strengthened their lungs and prevented them from being spoiled. She therefore calmly continued chatting with us while the baby's cries grew louder and louder. Finally, after ten minutes (apparently the requisite time period), she picked her up and fed and changed her.

One time we were vacationing with friends at a cottage on a lake. The crib was set up in a room downstairs, which had a covering over all the windows to make it dark. Our friend Annie put little 18-month-old Kathy down for her nap in that room. When Kathy awoke in a strange dark place with no one around, she was naturally terrified. She began to scream and cry for her mother. Unfortunately, Annie had received parenting advice from an "expert" who said that children must learn that their parents will not always come running when they call. Therefore, Kathy was left to sob alone for several minutes while she "learned" this important lesson.

A friend of Charity's had recently had a baby, so she went over to visit. Expecting to see the new parents fussing over their little miracle, she was amazed to see the baby lying on a blanket in the corner with several toys scattered around him. Being well-educated, progressive parents, they were "teaching" the child how to be independent and amuse himself so he wouldn't always expect to be entertained.

When we were pastoring a local church, Mark often had counseling appointments in his office at home. Frequently people would bring their children along, assuming, I suppose, that I would baby-sit since I had nothing else to do! Well, I didn't mind watching the children if they had brought along something to play with. We had no children yet, and therefore had no toys of any kind in the house. I was continually amazed at how many people never thought to bring along something for their children to do, however. Or even when we had families over for an evening, it was unusual for them to bring along activities to occupy the children. Then, when they became bored (as they surely would), the next few hours were spent hearing frequent admonitions by the parents to "sit still" and "behave yourselves" and "put that down" and "leave that alone" and "come over here" and "be quiet!" Is it really the child's fault that his behavior deteriorates in such circumstances?

We were soaking up the sun by the pool of a hotel in Florida while on vacation a few months ago. In the middle of the afternoon, a young couple arrived with their little boy of about four or five. They had just checked into the hotel and none of them were wearing swim clothes. Mom and Dad relaxed on the lounge chairs and prepared to unwind. Little Junior proceeded to explore the pool area and meet the other vacationers.

Before too long, however, the sparkling pool began to beckon, and the onslaught of whining began: "I want to go swimming! Why can't I go swimming now? I want to! You said I could go swimming when we got here! I want to go now! Please, please, please!" And, of course, the expected responses came, "No, you can't go swimming now. You don't have your suit on. We aren't dressed to take you in. You'll have to wait. Find something else to do for a while."

It apparently never occurred to them that there would be no relaxing for them (or for anyone else within hearing range!) unless they provided a fun activity for their son. Instead of caring for his needs, their wonderful vacation got off to an unhappy start with everyone snapping at everyone else and no one relaxing or having fun.

When our children were nine and eleven years old, we took an extended ministry tour that involved a great deal of flying. Although this was their first time in a plane, I knew that the novelty would wear off quickly and they would soon be bored. We therefore spent a few hours at Toys 'R' Us collecting small, inexpensive, quiet toys specifically for traveling. When we got home from the store, we packed them in the kids' carry-on bags to be saved for the trip.

What a lifesaver they were! Since it had been a few weeks between buying the toys and the trip, they had forgotten much of what they had chosen, so opening the bag on the plane was almost as good as Christmas. They were kept occupied and content throughout the tour (well, as content as any of us were during hours on a plane!). After the tour, these carry-on bags of goodies were kept in the car as designated "travel toys," and provided many hours of peaceful and pleasant car trips.

Maslow's Hierarchy of Human Needs

Dr. Abraham Maslow was a student of human behavior and motivation who is probably most famous for his theory on the "hierarchy of needs," which states that people will strive to fulfill progressively higher levels of need – from nourishment, safety, love and esteem to self-actualization. In the levels of the five basic needs, the person does not feel the second need until the demands of the first have been satisfied, nor the third until the second has been satisfied, and so on. Beyond these needs are higher levels of needs, including understanding, aesthetic appreciation and purely spiritual needs. In other words, if the most basic needs of our children are not met, they cannot successfully move onward toward becoming all that God intended them to be.

Maslow set up a hierarchy of five levels of basic needs, as follows:

1. *Physiological needs*: These are the biological needs for oxygen, food, water, warmth/coolness, protection from storms, and so on. These are the strongest needs because if deprived, the person could or would die.

2. *Safety needs*: Adults have little awareness of their security needs except in times of emergency or periods of disorganization in social structure. However, children strongly sense the need for safety and security, and often will display signs of insecurity and a need to know they are safe.

3. *Love, affection and belongingness needs*: Once the more basic physical needs are met, people seek to overcome feelings of loneliness and alienation. This involves the need to both give and receive love and affection and to establish a sense of belonging.

4. *Esteem needs*: People need both a stable, firmly based, high level self-esteem and the respect of others in order to

feel self-confident and valuable as a person. If these needs are not met, the person feels inferior, weak, helpless and worthless.

5.   *Self-actualization needs*: When all of the previous needs are satisfied, then the needs for self-actualization are recognized. Maslow described self-actualization as a person's need to be and do that which the person was "born to do." It is his "calling." A musician must make music, an artist must paint, and a poet must write.

You can immediately see the significance of these needs for us as parents. Our responsibility to meet the needs of our children, who are totally dependent upon us and who develop their perception of God from their perception of us, goes far beyond the requirements for food, clothing and shelter. We must also ensure that our children know that they are safe and secure in our care. We must enfold them in our love, shower them with affection and convince them that they are an essential part of our life and our family. We must respect them as unique creations of God, and lead them into a revelation of their true identity as His children, which is the only truly stable foundation for a healthy self-image. And finally, once these needs have been met, our children will begin to grow into the distinctive expressions of their Lord that He intended them to be.

You'll Spoil Them!

Soon after Charity was born, I obtained a little sign that expressed my motto:

> "Cleaning and dusting can wait 'til tomorrow
> For babies grow up, we've learned to our sorrow.
> So quiet down, cobwebs; dust, go to sleep.
> I'm rocking my baby, and babies don't keep."
> (Author unknown)

I was always reluctant to tell my friends or family how much time I spent rocking my children because I knew many of them would believe that so much attention would spoil them. They would (supposedly) never learn to go to sleep by themselves if I rocked them to sleep for every nap and before bedtime at night. But I didn't care. I didn't believe that a baby *could* be spoiled. Babies don't know about selfishness and manipulation. They only know about basic needs. My children go to bed on their own just fine, and have for many, many years, thank you very much! And do you know what else? I don't regret one minute I spent in the rocking chair looking down into those precious little faces. There is not one single thing that I wish I had done instead because I now realize it was more important.

But as I was preparing this chapter on respect, I was reminded again of those who believe that meeting all of a child's needs will spoil him. In order to decide if this is true, we first need to determine what a spoiled child looks like. We have all seen them and been appalled by their behavior and probably wanted to give them a good smack! But what was it about them that made us decide they were spoiled?

Is merely having all of one's needs met being spoiled? If it is, then our heavenly Father is guilty of spoiling all of His kids. *"For my God shall supply all your needs according to His riches in glory in Christ Jesus"* (Philippians 4:19). If God's parenting of us is the ultimate example of perfect parenting, then it seems that we *are* to meet all the needs of our children. If we do not do our very best to do so, how will they ever have faith that their heavenly Father wants to? How will they learn to trust Him when they grow older if they were not able to trust their earthly fathers and mothers when they were young?

Knowing that my God will meet all my needs makes me feel secure, safe, sheltered and protected. Knowing I have Someone on Whom I can depend gives me confidence to face whatever comes my way in life. Knowing that they can depend on their parents to meet all their needs will have the same positive impact on our children. It will develop an inner strength and assurance that will enable them to step out into an unknown world with poise and confidence.

So, what is a spoiled child? Does having a lot of material possessions make one spoiled? If so, then once again God is guilty of spoiling His children.

"Now Abram was very rich in livestock, in silver and in gold."
(Genesis 13:2)

"And the LORD *blessed [Isaac], and the man became rich, and continued to grow richer until he became very wealthy."*
(Genesis 26:12, 13)

"... And I will give you [Solomon] riches and wealth and honor, such as none of the kings who were before you has possessed, nor those who will come after you."
(2 Chronicles 1:12)

"Brethren, I pray that in all respects you may prosper and be in good health, just as your soul prospers."   (3 John 2)

From one end of the Bible to the other, God has promised and kept His promise to bless His children with abundant material prosperity. If the simple possession of material goods spoils a child, then it must be an accurate corollary that all rich children are spoiled, and no poor child can be. But if being spoiled is a characteristic of the child, then it can only be influenced by outward circumstances. It cannot be defined by them.

The Self-Centered Child

Now we are getting to the heart of what defines a spoiled child – it is something about the child himself; it is a characteristic of the child herself. It is not what is done to or for the child; it is not the outside influences that define a child as spoiled. Rather, it is the child's response to those influences. It is the child who will not accept the word, "No." It is the child who thinks only of himself and is uncaring of the feelings of others. It is the child who is wholly self-centered that we call spoiled.

Can meeting all of a child's needs cause him to become selfish and self-centered. Yes, of course it can. But must it? Does it automatically follow that the person who need not worry about having his needs met becomes egocentric? Again, we need only look at the fact that God has promised to meet all of our needs, yet He expects us to be loving and generous, to know that one must not necessarily follow the other.

So, how can we meet all the needs of our children without causing them to become self-centered? The most effective way I know of is to model concern for the feelings and well being of others. For example, whenever I would be away from the house for a few hours for a meeting or an appointment, Mark would watch the children. As the time grew near for my return, he always called on Charity and Joshua to help him clean up the house "as a love-gift for Mommy." Making Daddy's favorite dinner was always a special occasion. From the time they were very young and just beginning to receive an allowance, Chari and Josh learned the pleasure of picking out and giving personal Christmas gifts and travel souvenirs to their grandparents and special friends.

From their early teens, Joshua and Charity have jointly sponsored a child through Compassion International. Being involved with their homeschool group gave them the opportunity to help an elderly couple prepare their home for winter, and houseclean the home of a woman with cerebral palsy. You don't need instruction on how to show your children how to care about other people! Just invite them to participate with you as you do all the things you do for others. As you are respectful of your children and your parents and your spouse and everyone with whom you have contact, your children will understand that they are not the center of the universe, though they are one very important part of it.

Derek Prince defines biblical abundance as having enough to meet all your needs with some left over to share. That is how the Lord blesses us. It is much easier to be concerned about the needs of others when your own needs are fully met. Peter told the lame man, *"Such as I have give I thee"* (Acts 3:6). In Second Corinthians, Paul talks about his ability to give comfort to others because of the comfort he has received. Most courses on Christian counseling devote considerable time to healing the potential counselor before moving into training them. We can teach our children by example and by instruction to give out of their fullness to those who have need and to be sensitive to the feelings and emotions of others.

Just Mean "No!"

Another symptom of a spoiled child is his inability to accept the word, "No." It has been my experience that children will test those in authority to discover if they truly mean what they say and are willing to back up their words with appropriate actions. Once an individual has proven that "No" means "No," even to little Bobby, little Bobby will accept the prohibition.

Most often, if you see a child ignoring his mother's "No," you will soon discover that she didn't really mean "No" right at that particular moment. She may be the kind that automatically says, "No" to every request without thinking about it. Little Bobby has learned that if he keeps nagging and whining long enough, the "No" will certainly change to "Yes." So why should he accept the original "No"?

Or, she may be the kind that lies to her child, without ever even realizing that is what she is doing. For example, she may say, "Stop that right now or I'm going to leave you here in the store!" Or, "If you do that, a policeman will arrest you and put you in jail." Or, "Don't do that or you won't get any presents for Christmas." Little Bobby knows very well that none of those threats is ever going to be carried out, so why should he curtail his behavior based upon them?

The way to keep from raising spoiled children who won't listen when you say "No" is to say only what you mean and mean only what you say. We will be talking more about this in the next chapter, but suffice it to say at this time that thinking before you speak, saying only what you are willing to stand behind, then standing firm in what you say is a very simple solution to this problem.

Charity is one who has always loved a challenge. That means that if she was ever told, "You can't," she instantly had to prove she could. Telling her no was the surest way possible to make her want to do something. I know she is not alone in this tendency, for Paul talks about it in Romans 7:7–10,

> *"For I would not have known what coveting really was if the law had not said 'Do not covet.' But sin, seizing the opportunity afforded by the commandment, produced in me every kind*

of covetous desire . . . I found that the very commandment that
was intended to bring life actually brought death."   (NIV)

Charity is also strong-willed like her father, and I learned
very soon that her will was stronger than mine. However, it is
Mark's strong will that has given him the courage and ability
to press on into new areas, overcome obstacles, and become
the leader he is today. I had no interest in breaking Chari's
will. I knew that it was one of the greatest gifts God had given
her and that He would use it for His glory.

So how was I, a sensitive, fairly weak-willed person supposed
to train and discipline such a strong-willed child? If we were to
enter into a contest of wills over every little issue throughout
every day, I knew I would soon grow weary and give in,
perhaps on something on which I should have stood firm.

Therefore, I learned to choose my battles carefully. If there
was a way to accomplish my goal of keeping her from harm or
from harming someone else or from being discourteous, or
whatever my goal happened to be, without saying no, then
that was the route I pursued. If I could direct her attention
away from the potentially coveted object or activity to something that was acceptable, I did so. If I could challenge her *not*
to do something I didn't want her to do in such a way that it
was a fun game, that is what I did.

For example, we may be waiting on the sidewalk outside a
store for Daddy. The driveway and parking lot are right next
to the sidewalk, and I don't want Charity stepping off into the
path of a car. If I were to say, "Don't step off the sidewalk,"
instantly her attention would be focused on that forbidden
land, the parking lot, and her whole desire would be to visit it.
However, if I were to say, "Let's see how close you can walk to
this edge of the sidewalk (that is, the edge away from the
driveway) without stepping on the grass!" her focus is now
not on the forbidden but on the challenge. She will stay as far
away from the driveway as she can and be very happy to do
so. My goal has been met without a clash of wills, a noisy
scene or a dangerous dash into the traffic.

I expect some of you will be thinking, "You just need to
teach her to be more obedient. If you say no and she won't
accept it, strong and swift discipline will pull her in line."

Well, that is certainly one way to go, but it would not have worked for me, and Charity and I are both convinced it would not have worked for her. To this day, she recognizes within herself the resistance to any prohibition. Thankfully, her commitment to the Lord is stronger, and she obeys out of love for the Lord and me.

Taking portable quiet toys and books wherever we went was another way to avoid ugly scenes. When we visited other people's homes, I certainly did not want my children breaking their valuables or interrupting us constantly with whines about not having anything to do. Expecting a young child to sit still with nothing to occupy him for more than a few seconds is totally unreasonable. Joshua would spend hours listening to stories on cassette while looking at the books that went along with them. Coloring books are an old standby but still effective. A bucket of building blocks can hold a child's attention for hours. I encourage you to invest in special quiet toys that only come out occasionally, so they remain a treat. Your family will be much more peaceful, and your hosts will be very grateful!

So did I ever just say no? Of course I did. No one who has ever raised a child could possibly doubt that there were plenty of times when nothing else would accomplish my goal except a clear, "No." But by avoiding those unnecessary no's, I was more prepared to stand behind the necessary ones with firmness and resolve. I wasn't worn down by the incessant need to maintain my position of authority.

Respect Everyone In Every Way

Once again we turn to the theme of this chapter: "Honor all people; Respect everyone in every way." Respect your children as creations of your God, gifts of His love, expressions of His goodness. They are co-heirs with you of the grace of God. They are made in His image.

> "The Jews would not willingly tread upon the smallest piece of paper in their way, but took it up; for possibly, said they, the name of God may be upon it. Though there was a little superstition in this, yet truly there is nothing

but good religion in it, if we apply it to man. Trample not on any; there may be some work of grace there, that thou knowest not of. The name of God may be written upon that soul thou treadest on; it may be a soul that Christ thought so much of as to give His precious blood for it; therefore, despise it not."[3]

If you will not respect them for their own sakes, remember that you are training them how to relate to others by the way you treat them. Your children learn most of what they know about human interpersonal relationships from their observation of the relationships that take place on a daily basis within your home. What are you teaching them?

What Is the Lord Saying to You?

Take the time to meditate in the presence of the Lord on what has been said in this chapter. Ask Him to draw out for you whatever He wants you to especially hear right now. Allow the Holy Spirit to instruct and guide you in applying His will to your family life.

Have you been showing respect for your children? Have you been treating them as gifts given into your care by your heavenly Father? Do you respect their ability to hear from God? Do you answer them when they call, or expect them to wait for your convenience? Do you actively listen to them when they talk to you? Do you listen with just your physical ears, or are you tuned to their hearts and what the Spirit wants to say to them through you?

Do you answer their questions to the best of your ability? Are you willing to admit when you don't know something? If you don't know the answer, do you search for it together?

Have you honored your child's attempts at self-expression and self-individuation? Have you mocked their efforts or complained about their individuality?

Are you doing your best to meet *all* of the basic needs of your child? Have you been content to simply provide for their food, clothing and shelter, assuming that doing anything further would spoil them? Are your children secure in the knowledge that they are safe with you and in your care?

Do you frequently tell your children you love them, and demonstrate that love with physical affection? Do you know your child's love language (what is the most meaningful expression of love to him)? Do you express your love in his language? Do your children feel that they are a vital part of your family, that you would be incomplete without them, and that that they are very precious to you?

Have you taught your children who they are in Christ, so they can find their true identity in Him? Do they feel self-confident and valuable as individuals? If not, in what ways have you contributed to their insecurity? In what ways does God want you to help build them up in Him?

Do your children know that they have a holy calling upon their lives, that they were created to accomplish something great in the world and in the kingdom of God? Are you seeking the Lord together about how they should be preparing for their destiny?

How do your children respond when you say, "No"? If they resist you, is it because they know that with enough pressure, you will give in to their desires? Is it because they know that you don't really mean it but weren't really paying attention? Is it because they have a strong-will and see every prohibition as a challenge to be overcome? How does God want you to change so that your children will accept your "No" as your final word?

Have you made every issue, no matter how important, a contest of wills? Is the Lord asking you to change in any way? Would any of your children be considered "strong-willed"? How does the Lord want you to respond to their unique gifts?

Notes

1. David H. Albert. *Home Educators Family Times*, P.O. Box 708, 51 West Gray Rd., Gray, ME 04039. April 2001, p. 9
2. Biblesoft's New Exhaustive Strong's Numbers and Concordance with Expanded Greek-Hebrew Dictionary. Copyright © 1994, Biblesoft and International Bible Translators, Inc.
3. Coleridge; quoted in *Walking on Water* by Madeleine L'Engle, © 1980, 1998, Shaw, pp. 125, 126

Chapter 6

Watch Your Words!

"I'm having problems with my brother," complained our friend Susan. "He keeps giving my son Tommy a hard time just because he calls his little sister 'Fatty'."

"It doesn't bother you that he calls her 'Fatty'?" we asked in surprise.

"Nah," she said. "My family called me 'Fatty' all the time when I was growing up and it never hurt me any."

Shocked, we reminded her of the great damage done to her body by the bulimia she had suffered in her early twenties, including the loss of all of her teeth. Until we suggested the possibility, it had never occurred to her that there might be a relationship between these two incidents.

"There is one who speaks rashly like the thrusts of a sword ... "
(Proverbs 12:18)

"With his mouth the godless man destroys his neighbor ... "
(Proverbs 11:9)

" ... Perversion [viciousness] *in* [the tongue] *crushes the spirit."*
(Proverbs 15:4)

*"Death ... * [is] *in the power of the tongue ... "*
(Proverbs 18:21)

"So also the tongue is a small part of the body, and yet it boasts of great things. See how great a forest is set aflame by such a small fire! And the tongue is a fire, the very world of iniquity; the tongue is set among our members as that which defiles the entire body, and sets on fire the course of our life, and is set on fire by hell ... With it we bless our Lord and Father, and with it we curse men, who have been made in the likeness of God; from the same mouth come both blessing and cursing. My brethren, these things ought not to be this way."
(James 3:5–6, 9–10)

Words That Curse

Are you aware of the power that is in the words you speak to your children? As an authority figure in their lives, your words have the power to bless and the power to curse them. Your words, even spoken idly, without premeditation, and out of the emotion of the moment, carry with them the power to influence and affect the rest of your children's lives for good or for ill.

What do you say when your active little girl has knocked over her milk reaching across the dinner table for the third time this week? "You are SO clumsy! You are ALWAYS spilling something!"

How do you react when your curious little boy tries to help you in your shop but instead ruins an expensive piece of wood? "You're all thumbs! Can't you do anything right?"

As you listen to your seven-year-old trip over the simplest words in his reader, do you burst out in exasperation, "You'll never learn to read! What's the matter with you? Are you stupid?"

When your teenager spends hours exercising and carefully watches what she eats to try to become slimmer, do you exclaim in disgust, "You're just chubby! You've always been chubby and you always will be! Just live with it!"

After running out of gas on the expressway, do you burst into the house yelling, "Who's the dummy that didn't fill up the car? Why doesn't anyone else around here ever take any responsibility?"

Do you think it is funny to knock on your son's head when

he doesn't understand your explanations, like Biff did to McFly, saying, "Hello? Anybody home?"

Have you ever said anything like this to your children?

"You dummy!"
"You'll never make it!"
"You are such a loser!"
"What a moron!"
"You don't have the brains God gave an ant!"
"You never finish anything!"
"You're just fat!"
"You never understand anything!"
"You are so lazy!"
"You'll never amount to anything!"
"What a twit!"
"How can you be so stupid?"
"You are totally tone-deaf!"
"You have two left feet!"
"You are so dense!"
"What a wimp!"
"You're hopeless!"
"You are never going to accomplish anything!"

Do you ever talk about your children or introduce them with negative comparisons?

"This is my lazy daughter."
"He's the dumb jock."
"This is the computer nerd."
"She's the 'blonde' in the family, if you know what I mean."

What are your nicknames for your children? Loser? Dummy? Beanpole? Moron? Pudge? Piglet? Doofus? Fatty? Stinky? Tubby? Twit? Dingbat? String Bean? Goofy? Dum-Dum? Something worse?

Just as God created the world by the words that He spoke, He has given us the power to create with our words. The words we speak over our children carry a creative energy that creates the reality that we speak. Often we have counseled adults who are trapped in patterns of behavior that they recognize are destructive but from which they seem unable to break free. They carry beliefs about themselves that are totally contrary to who they are capable of being. These thought and behavior patterns can be traced directly back to words spoken by their parents or teachers when they were children. They have cut into their hearts like arrows where the poisonous tips have remained to infect their spirits.

The Curse of Poverty

Mark was raised in an extremely conservative church in which the ministers were men chosen from within the local church who maintained their "secular" vocations while serving as pastors. This didn't put too much of an extra burden upon them, however, since the church did not believe in studying the Bible (because "much study is a weariness of the flesh," according to Ecclesiastes 12:12), so they didn't need to devote any time to sermon preparation.

When Mark was called into the ministry at age 16, he was led to go to a Bible college for training (and as a result had the choice of dropping his membership from this church or being excommunicated. He chose to leave voluntarily!). However, one of the individuals who was in authority over him advised him to train for a more practical, secular job as well, since "it was unlikely that he would be able to make a living from the ministry." Given the religious climate of the community, this was an apparently reasonable assumption.

Mark's major source of income throughout our marriage has been the ministry. However, he has also always maintained other sources of revenue such as apartment rentals and sales. He developed an expectation that ministry activities could not support themselves financially, and therefore businessmen and women must come alongside to supply the extra money necessary to advance the kingdom. Our personal ministry income has always been very low. The church we planted (with approximately 150 adults as members) eventually increased our salary to a high point of $100 per week, plus our house and car. This provided only the bare necessities for a growing family of four, and we did most of our clothing shopping at the Goodwill.

In 1988 the Lord led us to launch out into a parachurch ministry whose mission was to saturate the world with the message of communion with God. We set our salary at the level it was in the last church at which we had worked. Mark began traveling around the world teaching seminars at churches that invited him to speak. We did not feel we should set a specific fee for his ministry but rather trust the Lord to provide through free will offerings. This would allow smaller churches to also benefit from his teaching.

Soon he was traveling at least two weekends each month within the States and four to six weeks per year in other parts of the world. Nearly all of his waking hours were spent in his office, studying, writing and counseling. Yet at the end of the week when the ministry bills were paid, there were many weeks when there wasn't enough left to meet our personal salary.

The ministry gradually grew, and after about ten or twelve years we were finally able to consistently receive our salary (which had not been increased during that time). However, we had many dreams and plans for the ministry that we were unable to fulfill for lack of money, and our personal indebtedness continued to increase.

Finally, the Lord reminded me of the words that were spoken to Mark as a young man, words that he had received into his heart and which had essentially acted as a curse upon our finances: "It is unlikely that you will be able to make a living from the ministry." Our family prayed together, repenting for believing a lie and not trusting God to bless us as He has promised. We broke the power of that curse over us and asked for the release of all that God had planned for us.

Immediately a change came upon our ministry. The month after our prayer, the ministry income was three times higher than it had been for the same month of the previous year! Since then, our income has continued to grow, we have been able to pay off all personal debts, and we have begun to see some of our dreams come into fruition.

Never underestimate the power your words, even your idle words, have to affect the lives and destinies of your children. Jesus Himself said, *"I say unto you, that every idle word that men*

shall speak, they shall give account thereof in the Day of Judgment"
(Matthew 12:36 KJV).

Words That Bless

> *"There is one who speaks rashly like the thrusts of a sword,*
> **But the tongue of the wise brings healing."**
> > (Proverbs 12:18)

> *"**A soothing tongue is a tree of life,***
> *But perversion* [viciousness] *in it crushes the spirit."*
> > (Proverbs 15:4)

> *"Death **and life** are in the power of the tongue,*
> *And those who love it will eat its fruit."*   (Proverbs 18:21)

On the other hand, we can use our words to our children to speak blessing, life and healing. Remember the importance that Jacob and Esau placed on their father's blessing, and the lengths they were willing to go to receive it? And with good reason, since the history of their descendants has been determined by the words Isaac spoke at that time. Nor is this an isolated incident. Throughout the Bible there are many records of the power of the father's blessing. It was expected that the Jewish father would bless his children, and his words carried such power that they could not be changed. Your words as parents carry the same power today to invoke a blessing upon your children.

Let's look at just a few of the blessings fathers pronounced over their children.

Isaac said to Jacob (believing it was Esau):

> *"Now may God give you of the dew of heaven,*
> *And of the fatness of the earth,*
> *And an abundance of grain and new wine;*
> *May peoples serve you,*
> *And nations bow down to you."*   (Genesis 27:28, 29)

Jacob said to Judah:

> *"Judah, your brothers shall praise you;*
> *Your hand shall be on the neck of your enemies.*

Your father's sons shall bow down to you . . .
The scepter shall not depart from Judah,
Nor the ruler's staff from between his feet,
Until Shiloh comes,
And to him shall be the obedience of the peoples."
(Genesis 49:8, 10)

Jacob pronounced to Joseph:

"From the God of your father who helps you,
And by the Almighty who blesses you
With blessings of heaven above,
Blessings of the deep that lies beneath,
Blessings of the breasts and of the womb.
The blessings of your father
Have surpassed the blessings of my ancestors
Up to the utmost bound of the everlasting hills;
May they be on the head of Joseph."   (Genesis 49:25–26)

What blessing does the Lord want you to pronounce on your children?

Words That Give Grace

*"Let no unwholesome word proceed from your mouth, but only such a word as is good for edification according to the need of the moment, **so that it will give grace to those who hear.**"*
(Ephesians 4:29)

The words that we speak in our homes and to our children can become important channels through which the grace of God can pour into their lives. We can speak words of encouragement and edification that will build up our child's faith, hope and love. We can influence their future for good by the words that we say to them now.

When they make a mistake, we can encourage them with a confidence that, with continued effort, they will be successful. By "encouraging" I do not mean what one of our friends considered encouraging her son with his schoolwork. Without any regret or embarrassment, she told us that she always "encouraged Justin to do his best on his papers." When he finished, if she thought he could do better, she ripped up his work and told him to start over. This does not promote **en**couragement but **dis**couragement! No wonder Justin found school very difficult and wanted to quit as early as possible.

In many homes, it seems to be easier for the mother to speak more positively to the children, while the father takes it as his responsibility to "toughen them up!" "They won't be mollycoddled in the real world, so they better not get used to it! My old man didn't cut me any slack and I'm a man's man today because of it. I'm not gonna pussyfoot around any kid of mine!" Any expression of kindness, gentleness or understanding is seen as an expression of weakness that has no place in their definition of manliness.

Yet the apostle Paul had a different view of the way a father should relate to his children. Anyone objectively viewing Paul's life and experiences could not possibly consider him weak in any way. Yet, when he spoke to his children in the Lord, he was careful to deal with each one of them as he believed a father should deal with his own children, exhorting and encouraging them, and testifying, to the end that they should walk worthily of God, who called them into his own kingdom and glory (1 Thessalonians 2:11, 12 ASV). The Greek word for "exhorting" in this passage doesn't mean commanding, insisting, or criticizing, but rather connotes inviting and beseeching others to a desired behavior. Likewise, the word for "encouraging" includes the ideas of consoling and comforting.

If we, as fathers, want our children to walk in a manner worthy of God who has called them, we will invite, beseech, encourage, console and comfort them. And we will "testify" to them, drawing them into a life of faith and obedience because of our testimony of the working of God's grace in our lives.

Love in Word and Deed

Proverbs 19:22 NIV declares, *"What a* [person] *desires is unfailing love."* That is what your children desire and need from you – your unfailing love expressed in word and deed.

Pastor Henry Wright is a nationally known speaker who ministers to Christian audiences on the subject of healing and wholeness of body and soul. He states that in an average seminar, 50–70% of the participants indicate they do not remember ever hearing their father say, "I love you." What a tragedy! Our adults are walking wounded, and many of them have no idea how to break the cycle of coldness, loneliness and rejection for the next generation. Dr. Wright believes, based on his extensive research, that 80% of autoimmune disorders are a result of rejection by one's father, husband or other significant male figure. We are a people desperate for unfailing love and acceptance.

Your children *need* to experience your love. They need to hear the words "I love you" from your lips often. And they must hear you say them in every circumstance, not just during discipline ("You know I am only doing this because I love you") but spontaneously throughout the day, in moments of joy and sorrow, when you meet and when you part. It doesn't matter if it makes you uncomfortable to say the words. Your children need to hear them, and you must put their well being above your comfort.

Furthermore, you must do more than say you love them. You must show your love for them in ways that are meaningful to them. Show it in time spent together, in making them a priority, in being willing to enter into their world. Don't always expect them to enter into your interests and your hobbies if they want to be with you. Share their interests and their lives with them. Demonstrate your love for them by really listening to them and taking them seriously. Be willing to look below the surface to hear what their hearts are feeling and trying to say. Listen with your heart, and hear the deep needs of their spirits.

Clothe Yourself with Compassion

> *"Therefore, as God's chosen people, holy and dearly loved, clothe yourselves with compassion, kindness, humility, gentleness and patience. Bear with* [your children] *and forgive whatever grievances you may have against* [them]. *Forgive as*

> *the Lord forgave you. And over all these virtues put on love, which binds them all together in perfect unity."*
>
> (Colossians 3:12–14 NIV)

> *"Speak evil of no one* [especially your own children], *avoid quarreling, be gentle, and show perfect courtesy toward all men* [and women and children]." (Titus 3:2 RSV)

> *"Be kind to* [your children], *tender-hearted, forgiving* [them], *just as God in Christ also has forgiven you."*
>
> (Ephesians 4:32)

Have you recognized your children as your brothers and sisters in Christ? Have you applied the exhortations of the Scriptures concerning your relationships with others in the body of Christ to your relationship with your children? Is there any reason not to?

Time to Hear from the Lord

We must cry out with the Psalmist:

> *"Set a guard, O Lord, over my mouth;*
> *Keep watch over the door of my lips."* (Psalm 141:3)

> *"For we all stumble in many ways. If anyone does not stumble in what he says, he is a perfect man, able to bridle the whole body as well."* (James 3:2)

We are so far from perfect; we do stumble in many ways. Our hearts are heavy when we hear the words we have so lightly spoken through the hearts of our children. Oh, Father, purify our hearts and set a guard over our mouths, we pray!

Ask the Lord to reveal to you any ways you have spoken a curse over your children. Let Him remind you of your reactions to their failures and weaknesses. Allow Him to let you hear your own voice as they hear you. Draw upon His grace to truly repent and turn from your sin. Humbly ask your children for forgiveness for your sins against them, and pray with them to break the power of the curses you have placed upon them. Be sensitive in the future to the guard the Lord has now placed over your mouth, and when He gently reminds you not to speak, be obedient.

Now ask the Lord in what ways He wants you to pronounce a blessing over your children. What names and nicknames has He chosen for them that He wants you to speak over them? How does He want you to respond to their failures and weaknesses? Are there any specific words of blessing that He wants you to pronounce at this time, as the patriarchs of old did?

Ask the Lord how often you have been telling your children that you love them, out loud, in words, with your own mouth. Don't assume you know; your perception of the truth may be inaccurate. If He tells you that you have not been consistent enough in speaking words of love, repent to Him and to your children. Become sensitive to His gentle reminders that now would be a good time to speak of your love.

Also ask Him if you have been showing love to your children in ways that are meaningful to them. Are you listening when they speak? Are you answering when they call? Are you polite and courteous? Are you meeting all their needs as you are able? Are you listening to their hearts, not just their words? Are you letting them into your world? Are you entering their world as much as they will allow? Are you making time with them a high priority in your life? Do you know what their "language of love" is, and are you diligent to express your love for them in the language that is most significant to them?

Finally, ask Him how He wants you to relate to them as your brothers and sisters in His Body. What will that mean to your relationship with them? What will that do to your attitudes toward them? How will that affect the way and the words you speak?

If you recognize that you yourself are a victim of a curse pronounced upon you by your parents, you can break free from that today. You can use the sample prayer given at the end of Chapter 1 to liberate you from its power.

If you are one of that majority of people who has not known a father's expressed love, I recommend that you seek healing for your heart either through counseling or by the ministry of the Spirit through the books recommended in the Bibliography.

Chapter 7

Focus on Strengths

One dark night, a wise old owl sat high in his tree, pondering the mysteries of life. He thought about "bird-kind," how wondrous it was, and how gifted. There were birds that could swim, birds that could fly, and birds that could run. There were birds that could sing, and birds that could talk. Some birds were so beautiful, they set the standard for color and style for the whole animal kingdom.

Then, being a wise bird, he thought some more. He thought about how tragic it is that not all birds have the ability to do everything that every other bird does, and he wondered why that is. Finally, he realized that canaries sing sweetly because they have been trained to do so from the moment they are born, and parrots learn while very young how to make the most of their beauty, but neither of them ever really excel in the physical skills of running or swimming because they are never taught! Ducks never talk because they have never been given the opportunity to learn. And ostriches have to learn to run fast because no one has ever taught them how to fly!

Suddenly, the wise old owl had a brilliant idea: If he could bring together all the young birds into one place, he could give all of them the training they needed to be well-rounded birds. He could help them all reach their full potential! He could bring forth a generation of gorgeous birds who could *all* swim and fly and run and sing and talk! At the Owl School for Birds, there would be no discrimination, no separatism, no inequality. Everyone would have the same opportunities, and therefore, every graduate would have the same abilities. Equality would finally come to the bird kingdom!

The next day, the owl called together representatives from all of the bird families and told them his wonderful idea. A few questioned the wisdom of the plan, but they were strongly overruled by the majority. The crows were delighted that their children would soon be singing as beautifully as the night-ingale. The emus were thrilled that future generations would no longer bear the burden of being looked down on as "flightless birds." The swans looked forward to seeing their young bring home the gold from the Olympic hundred-meter run, which had always been dominated by roadrunners.

There was near unanimous agreement that it would be much better for all of the children to be trained by the experts the owl would hire than by their parents, whose knowledge and abilities were limited and therefore would only limit their children. And there was a great deal of excitement about the possibility of sending off the little ones every morning and having the whole day to accomplish the things that were really important.

So plans were made, committees appointed, and teachers hired. Finally the big day arrived – the first day of bird school. Young birds of every description arrived bright and early, excited about the great opportunity before them. The day was spent putting everyone through a series of tests to evaluate what classes each student needed.

The ducks were found to be strong in swimming and flying, but needed extensive remedial work in running and singing. The canaries were judged to be quite lovely, good at flying, and exceptional singers, but definitely underachievers in talk-ing and swimming. The ostriches were outstanding runners, but quite deficient in nearly every other category tested. The teachers were appalled to discover that every single student in the school performed poorly in at least two of the test areas. Extensive remediation would be necessary to make everyone meet the average standards. The owl had obviously taken over the education of young birds just in time.

The next day, everyone went to his assigned class. All day long, ducks, swans, and geese could be seen waddling around the track, while their ostrich instructor paced behind them, yelling instructions to "Pick up their feet," "Bend their knees," and "Get the lead out!"

In the drama department, the peacock was teaching starlings, quail, and sparrows how they could use make-up made from the juice of berries to make themselves more attractive, while the parrot was fast losing patience with his hummingbird, whippoorwill and turtledove students, who simply weren't applying themselves to learning the fine art of speech. And over in the pond, the duck spent his entire day pulling his canary students from the bottom of the pond and administering bill-to-beak resuscitation.

Finally, the long day ended. Ducklings cried as they were finally able to soak their bruised and blistered feet in the cool water of the pond. Young ostriches spent the whole evening with their heads buried in the sand, ashamed to face anyone because of their terrible failure in flying class. The quail chicks barely made it home alive, their brightly colored make-up making them easy-to-spot targets for all their enemies. The poor little canary children had to walk all the way home because their feathers were still water-logged from swimming class. And the nightingales caught dreadful colds and had laryngitis for a week.

Seeing the toll Mr. Owl's school was having on their children, and truly missing the pleasure of teaching them themselves, the parent birds refused to send their children back. Instead, the ducklings and goslings became fantastic swimmers and successful contributors to their community. The ostriches and emus happily raced each other through the fields, becoming well-adjusted and productive members of their society. The quail rejoiced in their "dull" coloring and lived a happy and fulfilled life in their fields. The parrots and cockatoos showed off their splendid plumage and extensive vocabulary and found great satisfaction in their achievements. The canaries and the nightingales sang for joy morning and night, praising their Maker for the gifts He had given them.

And wise old owl went back to pondering the mysteries of bird-kind.

"Equal Opportunity" Has Become "Equal Outcomes"

Many years ago, I was worrying to the Lord because one of my children wasn't getting perfect papers in one of their subjects. (I can't even remember which one it was any more.) Anyway, because I was homeschooling, and homeschooling was so unusual in those days, I worried quite a lot about how well I was doing and how well the children were doing. And one day I was fretting to the Lord because they weren't perfect. He replied, "It is all right to be average in most things, as long as you excel in your area of giftedness."

What a relief that was to me! I don't have to try to make my children be the very best in every subject available. I only have to help them achieve adequacy in most subjects. It isn't necessary that they know everything there is to know in every area. It is only important that they achieve a level of competency that will provide a foundation for general success in life. It is more important that we focus on taking them as far as they can go in their areas of gifting and interest.

How contrary this is to the traditional American educational model. In our passion to provide equal *opportunity for* all children, we have attempted to create equal *outcomes from* all children. As a result, we have homogenized the education that all children receive, ignoring the fact that God made us with varying abilities and interests for a reason. Just as every part of the human body is shaped differently and functions differently than every other part, yet when they all work together in harmony there is perfect efficiency, so when every individual person does well what he is created to do and works in harmony with the rest of mankind, there is successful synergy. When we try to make everyone fit into a specific mold of abilities and skills, we rob our culture of the rich contrasts that individuality of expression can bring.

Our two children are as different from one another as two people raised in the same household can be. Homeschooling them presented challenges from both ends of the spectrum. Charity is a perfectionist. Every problem must be done correctly. Every paper must be perfect. A score of less than 100% on a test was cause for great sorrow and tears. My goal with her was to encourage her pursuit of excellence while at the same time convincing her that mistakes are an acceptable part of the learning process. Today, God is using Chari's attention to detail and commitment to quality for the benefit of our ministry, where she serves as our main editor and proofreader.

Joshua, on the other hand, was our dreamer. The amazing world around him was ever so much more interesting than the textbooks in front of him. While well able to think clearly and logically, he is also a gifted lateral thinker. You never know what tangent his mind will follow from a perfectly simple comment. It was easier for him to do math problems in his head than lay out all the steps on paper. Number "4's" were invariably turned into little sailboats. Today God is also using Josh's creativity and freethinking for the benefit of our ministry, where he serves as webmaster and market analyst.

Gifts That Differ

> *"Since we have gifts that differ **according to the grace** given to us, each of us is to exercise them accordingly ... "*
>
> (Romans 12:6)

> *"God has given each of us the ability to do certain things well."* (Romans 12:6 NLT)

Most commentators agree that in this passage Paul is talking about *all* the different kinds of gifts, talents and abilities that God has placed within people, for he includes such supernatural gifts as prophecy as well as the "natural" ones of giving, leading and serving.

> "All the endowments which Christians have are regarded by the apostle [Paul] as gifts. God has conferred them ... It may refer to natural endowments as well as to the favors of grace ... "[1]

> "Observe here how all the gifts of believers alike are viewed as communications of mere 'grace.'"[2]

> "The grace of God given to individual believers is shown in different gifts."[3]

The words in this passage for gift (*charismata*) and grace (*charin*) are actually related forms of the same root word. It is clear that the gifts that God has given to each of us to make us unique creations are one of the channels by which His grace flows to us and through us. Therefore, when we ignore, belittle or discourage our children's expressions of their gifts, we are building dams in their rivers of grace. And by encouraging and strengthening our children in their areas of giftedness, we are enlarging the conduits by which His grace can flow to and through them.

An Expert in His Calling

When the angel of the Lord came to Manoah and his wife and promised them a child, they had one question for him:

> "*Can you give us any special instructions about how we should raise the baby after he is born?*" (Judges 13:12 TLB)

> "*How shall we order* [govern] *the child, and how shall we do unto him?*" (KJV)

> "*What is to be the rule for the boy's life and work?*" (NIV)

In the same way, we must seek the wisdom of the Lord so that we may know how to raise our children so they may accomplish the destiny for which they have been created.

> "*Seest thou a man who is **expert in his calling**? Before kings may he stand;* [He will] *not stand before obscure men.*"
> (Proverbs 22:29)[4]

It is not necessary for an individual to be proficient in every possible discipline of life. It is only required that he be an expert in his calling! Then he can enter into the service of kings; he is entitled to claim the highest official post. He shall become a leader in this world because he is a skilled professional in the field of his calling.

But how does one come to this place of excellence? "*Train up a child in the way **he** should go [and in keeping with **his** individual gift or bent], and when he is old he will not depart from it*"

(Proverbs 22:6 Amplified). It is our responsibility to train up our children in the way *they* should go, in the unfolding of their talents and gifts, nurturing them and allowing them to flourish. It is "according to the tenor of *his* way, i.e., the path especially belonging to, especially fitted for, the individual's character. The proverb enjoins the closest possible study of each child's temperament and the adaptation of 'his way of life' to that."[5]

Matthew Henry translates this verse, *"Train up a child according as he is capable ... "* Only by hearing the Lord's special instructions for this particular child will we be able to train him in the way especially fitted for his character and his gifting and his calling. Only then will we raise children who do not fit into the customized mold of the rest of their generation, but who become the Albert Einstein's, the Henry Ford's, and the Thomas Edison's.

Thomas Edison is best known as the inventor of the electric light bulb. However, that is only one of the 1,093 inventions to which he held the patent. Truly he was an exceptionally gifted individual. Yet, after only three months in public school, he was asked to leave because his teacher had concluded that he was dull, addled and incapable of learning! How incredibly blind we can be to the unique gifts of our children!

Einstein could not manage lower math; arithmetic was too hard for him, and he made mistakes in his equations. Yet his mind could roam through the universe, unfettered, and he changed the foundations of our understanding of everything.

Henry Ford would have agreed with the interpretation of Proverbs 22:29 by the author of *Barnes' Notes*:

> "The gift of a quick and ready intellect is to lead to high office, it is not to be wasted on a work to which the obscure are adequate."[6]

Henry Ford's enemies were attempting to steal his company from him by proving he was mentally incompetent to run it. They took him to court, where the climax of his examination came when he was asked to recite his own telephone number and he was unable to do so! Believing they had triumphed, his accusers were put in their place when he explained, "If I need to call my home, all I have to do is press a button on my desk and one of my employees, who does know the number, comes running into my office to connect it for me. Why should I clutter up my mind with information that is useless to my work and which I have dozens of people around me capable of remembering?"

Although I would not recommend going quite to that extreme, I appreciate the principle he is endorsing. Especially considering the speed at which information and knowledge are increasing today, it is not only unnecessary, it is impossible to be an expert in very many subjects. During the Enlightenment, it was possible for some extremely gifted individuals to become what was known as "Renaissance Men." These people had studied all of the various disciplines of knowledge available in their day and were experts in every one. Since that time, there has been an explosion of knowledge.

Between the years 1500 A.D. and 1900 A.D., the world doubled the amount of information it had accumulated from creation up to 1500 A.D. From 1900 to 1975, the amount of available information was again doubled, in only 75 years compared to the previous 400 years. Between 1975 and 1985, knowledge and information doubled again, taking only 10 years. By 1993, it had doubled again, in eight years, and by 1998, only five years later, it had doubled again. At the beginning of this century, we have the potential to double the amount of information accumulated by mankind every ninety days!

Clearly, specialization is the only possible path before us. It is not reasonable to require the child who is not good at math to spend extra hours struggling to comprehend problems that he will never face again once he leaves the classroom. If a child delights in math and excels in its intricacies, he should be offered every opportunity to master it to the highest level of his ability, because he will probably use it in some way in his future. But the child that stumbles over the basic formulas of arithmetic will inevitably gravitate to a profession where higher maths are unnecessary and basic computations can be done on a calculator. Instead of making his education a time of drudgery and failure, why not discover what the poor math student loves and is gifted in?

Unless one pursues one of the history-related disciplines, there is very little need to memorize extensive facts and dates that can be easily discovered in reference materials. God has created every person with something special to minister to the world. Our purpose and goal should be to draw that out of our children and celebrate it with them.

I am not saying that there are no basic facts and skills that every student should learn and acquire. There is certain information that is necessary to be good citizens, successful Christians and productive members of society. But I believe that most of what is required beyond the elementary school level should be radically adjusted. Delight-centered learning should become the norm, where students pursue their areas of gifting and interest, one after another, until they develop their own particular gift-mix that will make a way for them to "stand before kings."

People who are successful leaders in the world are accepted and honored because of their strengths. Their weaknesses are not even considered. For example, what do we know about Mother Theresa's ability to do calculus? What do we know about Bill Gates' ability to spell correctly? What do we know about Albert Einstein's grasp of world history? What do we know of Billy Graham's science ability? What do we care? These individuals have shaped our world because of their *gifts*, not their weaknesses

Furthermore, as we become "experts in our calling," we shall move forward into greater levels of success. This increased success will call forth ever-increasing strengths in every area of our lives, even in previous areas of weakness. As we are successful, our achievements will create a demand for us to express a broader group of gifts in order to keep up with our unfolding accomplishments. As a result we will become obedient to our Lord's exhortation in Matthew 25 that we multiply our talents.

Why then do we have such an obsession to focus all of our time and attention on our children's areas of weakness – not just academically but socially and spiritually as well? Focusing on weakness creates depression, insecurity and inferiority. It prevents them from stepping forward in confidence to use their strengths. It creates a dam of hopelessness, failure and inadequacy in the channel of grace, stopping its flow into their lives.

Let's clear out those obstructions by building up our children in their areas of strength and gifting. Let's help them excel in their calling that they may become the leaders of tomorrow who stand before kings and shape our world.

Focusing on Spiritual Weakness

As devout Christians, we adults often make the same mistake with ourselves as we do with our children. We tend to fix our eyes on our own weaknesses and sins, struggling to overcome them, wrestling against the world, the flesh and the devil, overwhelmed by condemnation, discouragement and defeat. Our prayers are full of self-deprecation and remorse, begging for forgiveness and the power to overcome but never fully convinced that God can accept us because we are so full of sin and failure. Instead of drawing near to Him to be our strength, in our weakness and fear and guilt we withdraw from Him, half-expecting His righteous judgment to fall on us at any moment.

> *"Oh wretched man that I am! Who can deliver me from this body of sin?"* (Romans 7:24)

> *"Thanks be to God! ... There is therefore now **no condemnation ...** "* (Romans 7:25–8:1)

That is where God wants you to live today! You can live a life free from condemnation and guilt and despair. Take your eyes off your own weakness. Follow God's example in casting your sins into the sea of forgetfulness (Micah 7:19). *"Let us fix our eyes on Jesus"* (Hebrews 12:2 NIV)! As we do, *"we all, with unveiled face, beholding **as in a mirror** the glory of the Lord, are being transformed into the same image from glory to glory, just as from the Lord, the Spirit"* (2 Corinthians 3:18). When you look in a mirror, what do you see? Do you see your own faults, limitations and failures? Or do you see the One Who lives within you, Whose glory is shining forth to transform you *as you see Him within you!*

> *"For momentary, light affliction is producing for us an eternal weight of glory far beyond all comparison, **while we look not at the things which are seen**, but at the things which are not seen; for the things which are seen are temporal, but the things which are not seen are eternal."*   (2 Corinthians 4:17, 18)

You are transformed *as you gaze* on the invisible truth of the mystery that is the heart of Christianity: Christ is alive within you, changing you from the inside by His power and grace! You must not focus on your sins, which are but temporary aberrations. Instead you must fix your eyes on the invisible Christ Who lives within, Who is well able to live the holy life for which you yearn.

Some years ago the Lord gave Mark a simple but life-transforming revelation. He said, "Whatever you fix your eyes upon grows within you. Whatever grows within you, you become."

If you want to become sinful, fix your eyes on your sin. If you want to become impotent, fix your eyes on your weakness. If you want to be holy, fix your eyes on Jesus within you. If you want to become successful, fix your eyes on your gifts and what you love to do.

If you focus on your weakness, you will be full of fear, doubt, condemnation, self-pity, and hopelessness. If you focus on your strengths, you will be full of faith, hope, passion, and enthusiasm – everything that makes life worth living. Where will you fix your eyes?

As in a Mirror, Behold His Glory

Come to the One Who lives within you right now. Behold His glory. Worship Him for all that He is in you and all the gifts He has given to you.

Ask Him if there are any ways in which you have been focusing your attention on your children's weaknesses rather than their strengths. If He tells you that you have, wholeheartedly repent before Him, and your children if He so leads you.

Ask the Lord to reveal the strengths and gifts of each of your children to you, that you may see them as God created them. Make a list of the strengths of each child. Look at what you consider to be their weaknesses. Ask the Lord to show you possible ways in which He may use them as strengths. (Realize that He won't necessarily show you the future; He will only open your eyes to possibilities. Don't use what He shows you to put your children under bondage.)

Ask the Lord for a vision of the calling that He has placed upon your children's lives. Then ask Him to give you any special instructions about how you should raise each child. How shall you govern and train the child, and what will his manner of living be? Ask Him to teach you how to draw upon His grace so that you may be a channel of grace into their lives.

Where have you been fixing your eyes in your quest for holiness? Have you been focusing on your own sins and weaknesses? Have you been trying to overcome them with all *your* strength, neglecting to lean on the strength of the Lord and the power of His might? Do you see yourself as God sees you, clothed in a shining robe of righteousness, pure and holy with the holiness of the Son? Do you know that you have died with Christ and that sin has no more power over you? See the bibliography for suggestions of books that can help make this revelation real to you.

Notes

1. Barnes' Notes, Electronic Database. Copyright © 1997 by Biblesoft
2. Jamieson, Fausset, and Brown Commentary, Electronic Database. Copyright © 1997 by Biblesoft
3. The Wycliffe Bible Commentary, Electronic Database. Copyright © 1962 by Moody Press
4. Keil & Delitzsch Commentary on the Old Testament: New Updated Edition, Electronic Database. Copyright © 1996 by Hendrickson Publishers, Inc. Emphasis added.
5. Barnes' Notes, Electronic Database. Copyright © 1997 by Biblesoft
6. Ibid

Chapter 8

Make Them Your Ministry

"This generation, my generation, is badly in need of spiritual fathers ... We lack long-term vision. Fathers today need to be able to demonstrate how to dream for the long term. Ask someone my age for a long-term goal, and they'll tell you what they want to do next year. But a true long-term goal needs to be 5, 10, 25 years! Ouch, that's a stretch for most of us! I need to be taught how the race is a marathon and isn't a sprint.

I need to marry my zeal with your wisdom and both come out better for it, and I also desperately need to be taught to make quality decisions. But please, while you are telling us the right way, how about explaining how you arrived there? I think I need to learn the process, not just what the product should look like.

I realize that fathering costs you much more than teaching. The most memorable fathering experiences I have had with my dad are bike rides, games in the living room, a quick chat over coffee, not the classroom or the sermons. In the Hebrew school, disciples lived with the teacher and shared the experiences of life. The entire world became a blackboard with every arena teaching a new lesson. I am a sponge ready to soak up your vision and your lifestyle. If you share experiences with me, watch me catch your dreams and run with them.

I've heard the rumor that the young people will take the kingdom further than you have ever seen, but that bothers me. It seems to say, 'The older generation is done; they can move out of the way now.' The truth is, we'll actually regress without your help, your wisdom, your experience. The pride and spiritual elitism that have tried to invade the consciousness of zealous young people are traps and we don't want it. My dream is that as I enter my 40s and 50s, you and I and those I mentor would be ministering as a team: my fathers, my peers, and my sons. I don't need you to retire; now is your greatest hour. Let's build the kingdom as a team dedicated to humility and friendship. I'm waiting for your help.

Signed, – A son"[1]

I didn't plan to write this chapter. I thought I was finished with what the Lord wanted me to say and had the book completed without it. Then I realized that He had more He still wanted me to share.

Although I studied elementary education in college, I would not have considered it my calling in life. Of course, when I was young, those who influenced me did not talk much about calling or destiny. But looking back now, I see that going to college was the right thing for me to do, and studying elementary education was the right thing to do, but being a classroom teacher would not have been the right thing for me to do. I needed the confidence that the piece of paper saying I was prepared and qualified to teach children gave me. Without it, I may not have been bold enough to step out in homeschooling my children when the Lord told me to. (I hope I would have, but I was pretty timid in those days.)

Mark and I married while we were in college, and his calling to ministry was very strong. There was no doubt that he would give his life in full-time Christian service, which we understood at that time to mean either pastoring a church, being an evangelist, or moving to a foreign land as a life-time missionary. (We now understand that whatever a believer is called to do is full-time Christian service.)

When I married Mark, I knew that we would be working in a traditional church setting, and I understood that my ministry was to be a helper and support to my husband, standing alongside him and doing whatever he needed to make his ministry successful. For the first five years of our marriage, that meant studying together, attending meetings together, and doing all the little busy work things that go on behind the scenes. (I will never forget the mess of running a mimeograph machine! Thank God for Xerox!)

When Charity was first born, I continued much as before, just with the added paraphernalia that every baby requires. Her playpen was set up in our study and for about six months our lives went on as usual. Then, as she became more active, we began to recognize that my lifestyle was going to have to change. Supporting Mark's ministry evolved into caring for our children and providing him with a peaceful environment in which to grow and minister.

Not being a particularly social individual, I didn't fit into the stereotypical mold of preacher's wife. I wasn't interested in running any committees or leading any groups. Mark was a wonderful support to me, making it clear to our church that there was no biblical church position known as "pastor's wife" and that I was free to be who and what the Lord called me to be. He did not impose any expectations on me nor did he allow the congregation to do so. Therefore, I was free to seek the Lord's will for my life and obey Him without outside conflict.

During that time, I kept hearing the Lord whispering in my heart, "... *what shall it profit a man, if he shall gain the whole world, and lose his own* [children]?" (Mark 8:36). I don't know if the stereotype is true, but there is an accepted belief that the children of pastors and others in public ministry tend to rebel and bring sorrow and shame upon their parents.

There are many factors that could be blamed for this. The nature of ministry tends to make the family feel like they are living in a glass house, with everyone watching and judging their every move. Sometimes the children perceive the ministering parents as hypocrites, preaching one thing in public but living something entirely different in the home. And sometimes the "ministry" seems more important to the parents than their own children. Any scheduling conflicts between ministry events and family times automatically are resolved in favor of the ministry. The child feels that in the affections of his parents, he holds a poor last position. But where is the satisfaction of success in anything, if you have lost the love, respect, and honor of your own children?

The Lord made it clear to me that for at least the first twenty years of their lives, my children were to be my ministry. Just as God had called and gifted and anointed Mark for ministry to His Church, so He had called and gifted and anointed me for ministry to Charity and Joshua Virkler. As Mark was to devote himself to learning the ways of God and how to most effectively train the church in them, so I was to devote myself to learning and raising up these two children to be equipped and prepared for the destiny He had created them to fulfill. I understood this to be a temporary focus, a refining of my ministry of supporting and helping Mark by dedicating myself to raising his (our) children.

"I Don't See *That* Ministry in the Bible!"

You may be wondering what scriptural support I have for such a position. Especially in this day when women have been released from the bondages of tradition and domination, it seems anachronistic to suggest that it is a valid and high calling to make a home and raise a family.

I actually consider myself quite liberal-minded when it comes to gender roles. We have raised both of our children to believe that they can be and do absolutely anything, both in the Church and in the world. No position, no calling, no gift, no profession is closed to them because of their gender. The only factor that can and should limit their future choices is the voice of God within their own hearts. They can be anything – anything God calls them to be. They can do anything – anything God calls them to do. We just happen to believe that when God blesses you with children, He calls you to devote your life to raising them into strong disciples of Christ. And we do not consider this to be a detour or interruption from your "real calling." This *is* your "real calling" or ministry for this period of your life.

And I am not saying that it is only and automatically the mother who is called to the ministry of raising children. The majority of biblical instructions on parenting are actually addressed to fathers (e.g., Ephesians 6:4). I have observed a few families in which everyone would have benefited by their abandoning conventional roles and allowing themselves to think outside of their traditions. In some families, the father is the greater nurturer, the more merciful, the one more suited to the daily pressures of raising children. Each family must hear from God directly and personally what His will is for them.

Perhaps it would help to define what we mean by "ministry." The Greek word normally translated as "minister" simply means to serve. So, at its most basic, your ministry is the place where you serve the body of Christ. It is your calling; it is what you should be doing. It is the place where your gifts are called upon and anointed by the Spirit, and it is the place where God's strength is made perfect in your weakness.

So, with all the great needs of the world and the Church crying out for us to help, is it right for us to focus our time and attention on our own children who, after all, have all their needs met and are blessed simply because they are our children? When God called Abraham, He promised that He would bless the world through him. But that is not the reason He gave for calling him. Instead God declared, *"I have chosen him **in order that** he may command his children and his household after him to keep the way of the* Lord *to do righteousness and justice; in order that the* Lord *may bring upon Abraham what he has spoken about him"* (Genesis 18:19).

Above all the other reasons, God called Abraham so he would be a *father!* God called him to dedicate himself to raising and training and ministering to his own family and household. And if Abraham would devote himself to fulfilling this commission, then God would be able to keep all His promises to him, including blessing the world through him.

Have you noticed that the Bible is the story of a *family*? It is the record of the relationships and successes and failures of one family that became a nation, and of individual nuclear families within that larger extended family. When God made promises to people, He didn't promise to bless them and their church or them and their Bible study group or them and their ministry. He promised to bless them and their *children*.

God is interested in families. He has called and chosen us *in order that* we raise our children after us to keep the way of the Lord to do righteousness and justice, so that the Lord may bring upon us all the promises He has made to us! There is no greater ministry than our ministry to our own children and family. Perhaps if more of us were devoted to serving our children, we would find many of the other issues that seem to call out for ministry falling into order.

Paul exhorted the *"older women likewise are to . . . encourage the young women . . . to love their children"* (Titus 2:3, 4). I guess that I have now achieved "older woman" status, and in this book I am doing my best to instruct young parents how to love their children.

Relying on Your Gifts

We have said that your ministry is the place where your gifts are called upon and anointed by the Holy Spirit. If you look closely at Romans 12:6–8, you may be amazed at how many of the gifts of grace are necessary for the ministry of being a Spirit-anointed parent:

> *"We have different gifts, according to the grace given us. If a man's gift is prophesying, let him use it in proportion to his faith. If it is serving, let him serve; if it is teaching, let him teach; if it is encouraging, let him encourage; if it is contributing to the needs of others, let him give generously; if it is leadership, let him govern diligently; if it is showing mercy, let him do it cheerfully."* (NIV)

Let's look at each of these grace gifts.

Prophesying

According to 1 Corinthians 14:3, *"he that prophesieth speaketh unto men to edification, and exhortation, and comfort"* (KJV). When we prophesy, we speak words that strengthen, build up, encourage, comfort and console others. In our chapter on the power of our words, we talked about how important it is to speak only words that give grace to our children.

Serving

If anyone doubts that serving is a part of parenting, he obviously has never been a parent! Did you know that you can exercise your faith, and call on the grace of God to make your service to your children a ministry?

Teaching

Central to the biblical instructions to parents is the command to teach their children:

> *"And these words, which I am commanding you today, shall be in your heart; and you shall teach them diligently to your sons ... "*   (Deuteronomy 6:6, 7)

> *"Hear, O sons, the instruction of a father,*
> *And give attention that you may gain understanding,*
> *For I give you sound teaching;*
> *Do not abandon my instruction."*   (Proverbs 4:1, 2)

> *"My son, observe the commandment of your father*
> *And do not forsake the teaching of your mother;*
> *Bind them continually on your heart;*
> *Tie them around your neck.*
> *When you walk about, they will guide you;*
> *When you sleep, they will watch over you;*
> *And when you awake, they will talk to you.*
> *For the commandment is a lamp and the teaching is light;*
> *And reproofs for discipline are the way of life."*
>   (Proverbs 6:20–23)

Encouraging

Remember Paul's description of how a father speaks to his children?

> *"Just as you know how we were exhorting* [inviting, beseeching] *and encouraging* [consoling, comforting] *and imploring each one of you as a father would his own children."*
>   (1 Thessalonians 2:11)

Our heavenly Father is our example of perfect parenting, and when He speaks to His children, encouragement is at the heart of His words (1 Corinthians 14:3).

Giving (to meet the needs of others)

This is speaking mainly of financial sacrifice on behalf of another. Common sense tells us that it is the parents' responsibility to give whatever is necessary in order that the needs of their children be met. Paul reaffirms that, as believers, it is expected even more:

> "... for children are not responsible to save up for their parents, but parents for their children."
>   (2 Corinthians 12:14)

> "But if anyone does not provide for his own, and especially for those of his household, he has denied the faith and is worse than an unbeliever."   (1 Timothy 5:8)

Leading

God has placed you in front of your children (the literal meaning of the word translated "lead") that they may follow you as you follow Christ. As we live our life of faith before our children, inviting them to participate in our adventures with God and follow in our steps, they will try to be like us. Paul knew that children naturally imitate those whom they love, admire and respect (Ephesians 5:1). Therefore, he said to his disciples at Corinth,

> "I ... write these things to ... you as my beloved children. For if you were to have countless tutors in Christ, yet you would not have many fathers, for in Christ Jesus I became your father .... Therefore I exhort you, be imitators of me."
>   (1 Corinthians 4:14–16)

> "Be imitators of me, just as I also am of Christ."
>   (1 Corinthians 11:1)

Showing mercy

Again, we have talked earlier about the need to be compassionate and show mercy to our own children. But here Paul adds an extra instruction: We are to show mercy "with cheerfulness." This is not the grim judge who looks down from his lofty bench at the quailing offender and decides, out of his own great beneficence, to extend mercy. No, this word is related to the Latin *hilaritas*, which is the root of our English hilarity and exhilarate. When we show mercy to our children, it is to be with "the joyful eagerness, the amiable grace, the affability going the length of gayety, which make the [individual] a sunbeam ..."[2]

Clearly, whatever gifts we may have will be called upon as we give ourselves to the ministry of raising godly children. And all those gifts that we do not have become wonderful opportunities for God's Spirit to overlay us and perfect His strength in our weakness.

But Why Homeschooling?

By the time Charity was three years old, the Lord had further defined our instructions for raising our children to include teaching them at home. God had already led Mark into an understanding of journaling, and being able to clearly recognize His voice was an unbelievable encouragement to us. The decision to homeschool was surprisingly easy to make, considering that at the time it was unheard of. The Lord simply put it into our hearts as His purpose for us and there was never any doubt or question in either of our minds. The difficulty came in trying to explain what we were doing to our families and church members. We were blessed to have many schoolteachers within our congregation and it was a challenge to help them understand that our actions were not a personal insult to them but rather a step of faith in obedience to God.

There are many valid reasons to homeschool your children. In the past ten years, a wide variety of books have been written on the subject so I will not attempt to reiterate all they have to say. I would like to share with you, however, the Scriptures the Lord gave us to support His guidance. He made it clear that for the academic, social and spiritual well being of our children, homeschooling was the best possible choice.

Academic reasons
Jesus stated,

> *"I am ... the Truth"*   (John 14:6)

Paul said of Jesus,

> *"In Him **all** things were created, both in the heavens and on earth ... **all** things have been created through Him and for*

*Him. And He is before **all** things and in Him **all** things hold together."*   (Colossians 1:16, 17)

*"**All** things were made by Him and without Him was not anything made that was made."*   (John 1:3)

*"For from Him and through Him and to Him are **all** things."*   (Romans 11:36)

The Greek word for "all" in each of these passages is very specific, and literally means ... **all**!

*"The fear of the LORD is the beginning of **knowledge**."*
                                                   (Proverbs 1:7)

*"The eyes of the LORD preserve **knowledge**."*
                                                   (Proverbs 22:12)

And

*"in [Christ Himself] are hidden **all** the treasures of wisdom and **knowledge**."*   (Colossians 2:3)

All truth is God's truth. There is no truth in any area of knowledge or of life that is not traced ultimately to Him.

Each of these statements is as inclusive as it is possible to be. Jesus Christ is the *Source* of *all* truth, He is the *Center* of *all* truth, and He is the *Goal* of *all* truth. Therefore, any education that excludes Jesus Christ is deficient at its root, corrupt in its fruit, and can only be incomplete.

Further, God commanded us to love the Lord with all our mind (Mark 12:30) and to bring every thought captive to the obedience of Christ (2 Corinthians 10:5). Secular education cannot and does not train children how to do this.

It took us several years of concentrated effort after we finished college to bring the Lordship of Jesus Christ into the many areas of living that we had previously segregated from our Christianity. Homeschooling gave us the opportunity to continue that quest. What a joy it was to learn history from a biblical, spiritual viewpoint, seeing God raising up and destroying nations, preserving and judging His people, recognizing that "the Most High is Ruler over the realm of mankind" (Daniel 4:17).

Science is a major legal battleground where humanism and Christian faith have tangled. Instead of the "vain babblings" of unproven theories (1 Timothy 6:20), science for us was a worshipful experience, viewed as a study of the great Creator and how He has revealed Himself in His creation.

> "The heavens are telling of the glory of God;
> And their expanse is declaring the work of
>   His hands." (Psalm 19:1)

> "When He imparted weight to the wind,
> And meted out the waters by measure,
> When He set a limit for the rain
> And a course for the thunderbolt,
> Then He saw it and declared it;
> He established it and searched it out."
>   (Job 28:25–27; see also Job 37, 38 and 39)

> "From the breath of God ice is made,
> And the expanse of the waters is frozen.
> Also with moisture He loads the thick cloud;
> He disperses the cloud with His lightning.
> It changes direction, turning around by His
>   guidance,
> That it may do whatever He commands it
> On the face of the inhabited earth.
> Whether for correction, or for His world,
> Or for loving kindness, He causes it to happen."
>   (Job 37:10–13)

Literature was studied from a biblical perspective and philosophies judged by the only true standard. Art and music were seen as exciting ways to express and enhance worship and give substance to that which the eye of faith can see.

Jesus is Lord! He is the Lord of all truth and He wants to be Lord of our education. We are warned against receiving the teaching of the unrighteous. In the Old Testament we are exhorted, *"Cease, my son, to hear the instruction that causeth to err from the words of knowledge"* (Proverbs 19:27). In the New Testament, Paul instructed His disciple Timothy,

> *"Guard what has been entrusted to you, avoiding worldly and empty chatter and the opposing arguments of what is falsely called 'knowledge' – which some have professed and thus gone astray from the faith."* (1 Timothy 6:20, 21)

As Christians, it seems to me that the only valid education is one with Christ at its center.

Social reasons

> "If there were no other reason for wanting to keep kids out of school, the social life would be reason enough ... the social life of the children is mean-spirited, competitive, exclusive, status seeking, snobbish, full of talk about who went to whose birthday party and who got what Christmas presents and who got how many Valentine cards and who is talking to so-and-so and who is not. Even in the first grade, classes soon divide up into leaders (energetic and – often deservedly – popular kids), their bands of followers, and other outsiders who are pointedly excluded from these groups."[3]

These are the words of homeschooling advocate John Holt, who was a devout humanist with no interest in Christian values. Yet even he recognized that the social life of the public school (or any age-segregated gathering of children) promotes the most selfish attitudes and non-Christian actions. Why are Christian parents so slow to recognize this truth?

The Scripture is full of exhortations against finding companionship or even spending time with the ungodly.

> *"He who walks with wise men will be wise,*
> *But the companion of fools will suffer harm."*
> (Proverbs 13:20)

> *"Do not be envious of evil men,*
> *Nor desire to be with them;*
> *For their minds devise violence,*
> *And their lips talk of trouble."* (Proverbs 24:1, 2)

"You shall not follow a multitude in doing evil ... You shall make no covenant with them ... They shall not live in your land, lest they make you sin against Me ... "
(Exodus 23:2, 32, 33)

"Depart now from the tents of these wicked men and touch nothing that belongs to them, lest you be swept away in all their sin."
(Numbers 16:26)

"How blessed is the man who does not
walk in the counsel of the wicked,
Nor stand in the path of sinners,
Nor sit in the seat of scoffers!"
(Psalm 1:1)

"I hate the assembly of evildoers
And I will not sit with the wicked."
(Psalm 26:5)

"Depart from me, evildoers,
That I may observe the commandment of my God."
(Psalm 119:115)

"One sinner destroys much good."
(Ecclesiastes 9:18)

"Now I urge you, brethren, keep your eye on those who cause dissensions and hindrances contrary to the teaching which you have learned, and turn away from them. For such men are slaves not of our Lord Christ but of their own appetites; and by their smooth and flattering speech they deceive the hearts of the unsuspecting."
(Romans 16:17, 18)

"Do not be deceived: 'Bad company corrupts good morals.'"
(1 Corinthians 15:33)

If these commands apply to us as adults who are strong in our convictions and secure in our faith, how much more do they apply to our children who are still tender in their spirits, easily influenced by the voice of authority, readily swayed by the power of peer pressure? Skeptics of homeschooling usually point to the lack of social contacts as one of its drawbacks. Yet, as Christians, the opportunity to protect our children from the teaching of the ungodly and the company of the unrighteous is one of the greatest benefits we see to educating our children at home.

There seems to be an assumption that the age-segregated interaction that takes place in a school setting will produce social adaptability and poise. I am living proof that such a supposition is false. I attended 12 years of public school and four years of Christian liberal arts college, yet for many years I was shy, introverted, and barely able to carry on a conversation with a good friend, to say nothing of the frozen terror of meeting a stranger.

My children, on the other hand, who have been home-schooled throughout their lives, are totally secure and capable of facing any situation with confidence and friendliness. To be truly at ease with others is not the result of the artificial environment of the classroom. Instead, one must be at ease with himself and his God. If one has a strong relationship with the Lord, self-confidence and security come also. Out of these comes the ability to relate constructively with others.

(**Note**: Socialization is very different from evangelism. Our goal is not to isolate our children, but to strengthen them in their faith to the point where they are the ones who influence rather than the ones who are influenced by their peers.)

Spiritual reasons

"I am much afraid that the schools will prove the very gates of hell, unless they diligently labor in explaining the Holy Scriptures, and engraving them in the hearts of youth. I advise no one to place his child where the Scriptures do not reign paramount. Every institution in which men are not unceasingly occupied with the Word of God must be corrupt."   (Martin Luther)[4]

"... The battle for humankind's future must be waged and won in the public school classroom by teachers who correctly perceive their role as the proselytizers of a new faith: A religion of humanity ... utilizing a classroom instead of a pulpit to carry humanistic values into whatever they teach ... The classroom must and will become an arena of conflict between the old and the new – the rotting corpse of Christianity, together with all its adjacent evils and misery, and the new faith of humanism ..."   (John J. Dunphy in *The Humanist*)[5]

The current generation of teachers was trained in colleges and universities that have been deliberately and systematically infiltrated by zealous missionaries for the religion of humanism. Only those who knew the Word of God and were led by the Spirit of God were able to recognize the lies they were taught, and resist the pressure to embrace them. The philosophy of public education today is saturated with the doctrines of secular humanism, and we are reaping the disastrous results.

God has given us an alternative. We do not need to submit our children to the teaching of a different religion and a foreign god. We can take personal responsibility for the education and training of our children in the way of the one true God.

Perhaps the best-known (and – dare I say it? – least-obeyed) parenting instruction God has given is found twice in the book of Deuteronomy:

> *"And these words, which I am commanding you today, shall be in your heart; and you shall teach them diligently to your sons and shall talk of them when you sit in your house and when you walk by the way and when you lie down and when you rise up. And you shall bind them as a sign on your hand and they shall be as frontals on your forehead. And you shall write them on the doorposts of your house and on your gates."*
> (Deuteronomy 6:6–9; see also Deuteronomy 11:18–21)

How can we possibly fulfill this command if we send our children off to be trained and socialized by the unrighteous for half of their waking hours? How can we teach God's Word to them as we walk by the way if our children are not walking by the way with us?

Statistics indicate that the average father spends less than 15 minutes in personal conversation with his children each day. How can he possibly be an obedient parent in such circumstances? And the lives of mothers today are not much better. Between work and carpooling and housekeeping and church services and volunteer work, she has very little time to devote to her children, either. Do we really expect to raise godly children in the few stolen moments that we are willing or able to give them?

And how shall we help our believing children obey these injunctions?

> *"Hear, my son, your father's instruction*
> *And do not forsake your mother's teaching;*
> *Indeed they are a graceful wreath to your head,*
> *And ornaments about your neck."*   (Proverbs 1:8, 9)

(This is a recurrent theme throughout the book of Proverbs.)

> *"Cease, my son, to hear the instruction that causeth to err from the words of knowledge."*   (Proverbs 19:27 KJV)

> *"Guard what has been entrusted to you, avoiding worldly and empty chatter and the opposing arguments of what is falsely called 'knowledge' – which some have professed and thus gone astray from the faith. Grace be with you."*
> (1 Timothy 6:20, 21)

The Lord made it clear to us that our children were to be my ministry, and that we were to homeschool them. Let me share a portion of my journaling with you:

> "I do not want My children tarnished by the world ... When I called My people Israel, I commanded them to stay away from the pagan and ungodly. I did not want their influence corrupting the purity I was producing. It is still My desire for My people to be separate and untouched by the world. And how can a child, whose mind is so moldable and trusting, not be touched by an adult who spends six hours each day exerting her influence over her? You have seen how subtle and deceptive the enemy will be ... It is not My will for My children to be under such influence."

The Scripture the Lord was referring to in this journaling is the instructions God gave to Moses concerning the taking of the Promised Land. He said,

> *"In the cities of the peoples that the Lord your God is giving you as an inheritance, you shall not leave alive anything that*

breathes. But you shall utterly destroy them ... in order that they may not teach you to do according to all their detestable things which they have done for their gods so that you would sin against the Lord your God." (Deuteronomy 20:16–18)

And in the New Covenant, we hear similar words:

"Do not be bound together with unbelievers; for what partnership have righteousness and lawlessness, or what fellowship has light with darkness ... Or what has a believer in common with an unbeliever? Or what agreement has the temple of God with idols? For we are the temple of the living God, just as God said ... 'Therefore, come out from their midst and be separate,' says the Lord, 'and do not touch what is unclean; And I will welcome you." (2 Corinthians 6:14–17)

My Children Are My Ministry

I did not intend to promote homeschooling in this book. I love homeschooling and am grateful beyond words for the Lord's leading us into it so many years ago. But I have always shied away from saying that homeschooling was for everyone. I knew it was for me, but I always encouraged other parents to seek the Lord for themselves and be obedient to His leading, which I assumed might not be homeschooling.

However, as I have been writing this book, I have found my position changing. I have been looking more closely at the families we know, watching both children and parents and their interaction together, and I have noticed many things. And I have been earnestly praying for wisdom and insight, that I would say everything God wanted me to say and nothing but what He wanted me to say.

First, I have been struck by the faces of homeschooled children. Nearly all of them reflect a purity and innocence one would expect to find only in the very young today. Occasionally, there are those who have chosen to dabble in the things of the world, and their countenances are more like those of the Christian young people who have attended school. There is a mixture there; they are not cold and rebellious like the unbeliever, but there is a hardness, a "worldly-wiseness" that shows itself on their faces. I don't know if I am expressing myself well, but that has been my observation.

Then I wondered about those homeschooled children who have chosen to experiment with worldly pleasures. They hadn't turned away from God completely, but they had rejected some of the principles and rules that had been instilled by their parents. I wondered if it was because there had been too many rules, if they had been raised under law rather than grace and that had awakened their sinful natures.

But then I observed other homes where there were even more rules and regulations, yet the children continued in joyful submission and obedience. In fact, these children who had been taught an abundance of laws seemed to respond to their parents as our children responded to us. Their obedience was not out of fear of punishment but out of love and honor for their parents. Even though they could not personally justify some of the rules that they had been taught, still they embraced them willingly because of their respect for their parents and their desire to please them.

As I pondered and prayed about these families, I believe the Lord showed me the key. Although our philosophies of child-rearing could not have been more different, there was one point of common ground: in each family, the mother had embraced raising the children as her ministry. She was wholly devoted to serving the Lord and her husband by preparing her children for the destiny to which they were born. When the children were young and needed much of her time, she did not have any outside ministry or job. Usually she had a hobby to relax her and feed her spirit, but its importance was clearly secondary to her children's needs. As they grew older, she accepted volunteer work during church services, but it was always understood that her children and their needs were her primary priority (after, of course, her personal relationship with God and her husband).

I know it is possible to raise Christian children without making them your ministry or homeschooling them. But I am absolutely convinced that *these are major channels by which the grace of God can come flooding into your home*. I am not saying it is easy. It means laying aside some of your own desires and dreams, at least for a time. It may mean less money and less stroking of your ego. It will surely mean days of frustration and exhaustion. But it will also mean days of joy and laughter, discovery and beauty, creativity and exploration. It can be the most exciting adventure of your life!

My children are grown now, and the Lord is leading me into new ministries. I am not yet fifty years old, so I have at least another thirty years to accomplish the rest of my dreams. All that I have done for the last 25 years has been preparing me for my future, as well as Charity and Joshua for theirs. I am not the person I was when I began the homeschooling journey, thank God! I have grown at least as much as my children have, and God has worked in me as well as in them. I am much better prepared for whatever God wants for me than I was as a young person, and I am looking forward with great anticipation to the next season of my life.

What about You?

What do you think? Have I gone too far? Have I stepped over the line and offended you? I hope not. I hope I have challenged you to humbly seek the Lord's will for your life and your family, acknowledging that it may not be what you would have chosen but that it will be what is best for all of you.

Do you think raising children is a valid ministry to which a parent should devote him/herself? Have you considered raising your children to be a ministry? What is the Lord saying to you about it now?

Have you ever considered homeschooling? Are you willing to ask the Lord if it is what He wants you to do, and if it is, draw upon His grace to do it?

Perhaps you are feeling the gentle tug of the Spirit toward homeschooling, but your soul is sending out frantic objections. "We need two incomes! We can't possibly survive on just one salary!" "I'm a single parent. How could I possibly homeschool?" "I dream about the first day of school when the kids are out of my hair and I can have some time to myself! I couldn't stand being with them all the time."

"I didn't even graduate from high school! There is no way I am adequate to teach my children."

Whatever your objections may be, Jesus has the answer. Where God guides, He provides. If He calls you to home-school your children, He will supply whatever you need to be successful. You may need to make some sacrifices. You certainly will need to grow in grace yourself. But isn't that what Christianity is all about? Are you willing to step out in faith, trusting the Lord to be all that you need, as you are wholeheartedly obedient to Him?

I know there are situations where it seems that home-schooling would be absolutely impossible, and I admit I do not have the answers for you if you are in one of those situations. However, I do know that if God leads you into homeschooling, He will make it possible. *He* will find a way for you. Are you willing to step out into the Red Sea and trust Him to divide it that you may go forward on dry ground? Are you willing to trust Him?

In her book, *Quiet Moments for Homeschool Moms and Dads*, Vicki Brady shares the same fears you may have:

> "I've heard these same concerns expressed by other parents as well: What if my children do not learn? Will they fall behind other children? Can I afford the books? What will my friends think? How will my family respond? Will Social Services take my children? Will my children be able to go to college? Will they know how to play with other children? What if I don't understand the books? What if they want to learn calculus?
>
> Each time one of these fears surfaces, I like to picture the Son and Father having a conversation in heaven.
>
> 'Father, You've called this family to homeschool, but there seem to be problems. I don't think the mom is qualified – her children will end up way behind, unable to catch up. Maybe they'll wind up in a foster home.'
>
> 'Son, You're right. There's another snag, too. I forgot to arrange for the financing, so they will have to wing it without books. By the way, did You prepare their friends and family for this decision?'
>
> 'Me? I thought You covered that!'

When I imagine this heavenly conversation, it always puts a smile on my face. God knew exactly what He was doing when He called us to homeschool our children. Fear not, because our human strength will have nothing to do with our success. Success will come by His Spirit."

If you are jointly raising your children, I encourage both parents to pray about homeschooling. A unified acceptance of the call to this ministry will make the years ahead much easier for everyone. Refer to the Bibliography for a list of books that will encourage you in your journey. Bless you as you explore this exciting opportunity!

Notes

1. *Spread the Fire*, Issue 4, 2002, Toronto Christian Airport Fellowship, Toronto, ON, p. 6
2. *Vincent's Word Studies of the New Testament*, Electronic Database. © 1997 by Biblesoft
3. *Teach Your Own* by John Holt. Delacort Press, © 1981; pp. 44–45
4. Martin Luther, *What Luther Says Volume I*: p. 449
5. John J. Dunphy, Prize Winning Essay in *The Humanist*, Jan./Feb. 1983

Chapter 9

Release Them in Faith!

Mark and I were filled with the Holy Spirit and began moving in charismatic circles in the early 1970s. We were blessed to be exposed to the marvelous teaching of a group of anointed men known affectionately as "the Fort Lauderdale Five." The theology of these great men has been the foundation upon which we have built our lives and ministry.

However, one of the important truths that God restored to the Protestant Church through them was twisted by the enemy to bring heartache and shipwreck to many believers. I am referring, of course, to the discipleship movement. In case you missed that particular troubled time in Church history, I will briefly recap what I believe happened.

One of the issues which Protestants (rightly) protested against in the Roman Catholic Church was the excessive amount of authority endowed in the church leadership, and the doctrine that individual believers, the laity, were unable to hear from God directly. Traditional Protestant churches had therefore encouraged their adherents to study the Scriptures for themselves and be obedient to their own consciences in matters of their spiritual lives. This was a largely successful arrangement for many years, and believers of similar interpretations of the Bible gathered together for worship and study.

However, when the Lord poured out His Holy Spirit in repeated waves during the twentieth century, believers suddenly found themselves with another avenue of knowing truth – by the Spirit. This is a much more subjective standard than the written Word, and suddenly many strange and weird doctrines were being put forth in charismatic circles. "Thus saith the Lord" became a mantra against which it was extremely difficult to contend, for who is man to disagree with God? "Lone Ranger Christians" with their "God and I don't need anyone else" attitude dotted the spiritual country-side. Personal "revelations" and interpretations threatened to bring the charismatic renewal to an embarrassing end.

Into this state of affairs God spoke the truth of submission, that His Word is not of any private interpretation but we are all members of a body who need one another to function appropriately. In the Old Covenant, God's Spirit came upon individual men like Moses and spoke His word to them, and the rest of His people were expected to simply accept that the word came from God on faith. It was not necessary that they agree with it or understand it or confirm it. They were simply to obey.

However, in the New Covenant, God's Spirit is within and upon His entire body of people. When one prophet speaks today, the others are to judge (1 Corinthians 14:29). Each of us has the same Holy Spirit within him, and He will affirm the truth within us when we hear it, if we have a humble, teachable, obedient heart. Jesus promised that the Spirit of truth would dwell with us and be in us (John 14:16, 17), and that He would guide us into all truth, even truths that Jesus had not been able to speak of to His disciples (John 16:12, 13). When we hear truth, the Spirit of truth within us will leap. Of course, we always have the choice of whether we will accept His confirmation or not (whether we will be obedient or not).

So the Fort Lauderdale Five began to teach that it was necessary to submit the revelations we received from the Spirit to other mature individuals in the Body of Christ for their confirmation and adjustment. So far, so good. Unfortun-ately, the enemy began almost immediately to twist this truth to bring God's people under bondage. Not only were revela-tions to be submitted, but good disciples would bring every aspect of their lives under the authority of another. Every decision had to be made with the oversight of one's "pastor," who could be anyone who enjoyed wielding such power.

We personally knew a young couple who traveled with their children to another state to be "discipled." They moved into the home of their teacher and became virtual servants. They were no longer able to make decisions concerning the care and discipline of their children, and they were expected to serve their teachers in whatever way they were asked. Somehow, this abdication of their own personhood and responsibility was supposed to make them better disciples of the Lord. Lines of "spiritual authority" were established whereby a prominent, high-level individual would be allowed to make very personal decisions for a disciple on the other side of the country whom he had never met. Countless lives were ruined and untold numbers of believers left the faith because of the abuses of authority and power that the enemy was able to twist out of the truth of authority and submission.

Around the same time, but in totally different Christian circles, Bill Gothard was presenting his seminar on "Basic Youth Conflicts" to packed halls of conservative evangelicals. He was also teaching the value of submission, although his emphasis was within the family. Young Christians were encouraged to remain submitted and obedient to their parents, even unbelieving parents, until the parent-child relationship was replaced by the marriage relationship. *"The king's heart is like channels of water in the hand of the* LORD; *He turns it wherever He wishes,"* declares Proverbs 21:1. We can therefore be confident that God will work through the authorities in our lives to bring to pass His perfect will for us.

> *"For there is no authority except from God, and those which exist are established by God. Therefore whoever resists author- ity has opposed the ordinance of God; and they who have opposed will receive condemnation upon themselves."*
>   (Romans 13:1–2)

When the Lord gave Mark the message of communion with God and the keys that have helped so many of His people begin to recognize His voice within them for themselves, we recognized that there would be a need for some sort of accountability and methodology to help people judge whether what they were hearing truly was the Lord. Frankly, up until that time, many of the people we had heard declare, "God told me ..." were "granola Christians" – fruits, nuts and flakes! We didn't want the ministry that God had entrusted to us to be responsible for a proliferation of charismatic follies. We therefore carefully examined all the teaching out there on authority, submission, discipleship, and such related issues. We felt that what we taught as a result was a balanced approach.

We drew much from the teaching of Bill Gothard, being convinced, as he is, that God has established authority and He will work through it to accomplish His purposes for the world and for us as individuals. We especially appreciated his principles for disagreeing with authority, based on the life of Daniel. Submission did not involve our becoming doormats with no mind or will or revelation of our own. Instead, it involved a dialogue between two (or more) people who all had the Spirit of Christ within them and who could corporately come to truth. However, if consensus could not be reached, we believed that you should not act on what you believed you had heard from the Lord.

We taught and lived these principles for many years, and they protected us from making several major errors in our lives. However, the Lord has gradually been bringing a change in our thinking. Essentially, it boils down to the fact that, if you believe the Lord has told you to do something and you do not do it, for you it is sin. Even if you are mistaken in your belief about what God has said, if you have a pure, humble heart that only desires to do God's will, if you *believe* God has spoken, you must obey or you are being disobedient. Whatever is not of faith is sin (Romans 14:23).

*"So then every one of us shall give account of **himself** to God"* (Romans 14:12 KJV). On judgment day, God will not accept the Nuremberg Defense: "I am not guilty because I was only obeying orders." Just as we cannot accept such a feeble excuse for the atrocious sins that were committed during the Holocaust, neither will God accept such an excuse for our sins. We must each give an account of ourselves to God. We will be responsible before Him if we choose to obey man rather than God.

We therefore now see submission as a dialogue among equals. We continue to have two or three people to whom we consider ourselves submitted. That means that if we hear anything from God that we are unsure about, we share it with them and ask them to pray about it as well. If they are not convinced that it is the Lord, we continue to pray and discuss it together, hoping that we will come to corporate peace. However, the ultimate responsibility for our actions remains with us. If we eventually come to the place where we are convinced in our own hearts that God has spoken, we must be obedient to that, even if no one else agrees with us.

I should say, however, that we have never come to that place. Because each of those involved (us and those to whom we submit) has the same Holy Spirit living within them, that Holy Spirit has faithfully made His truth clear to all of us corporately. We have never had to go against what our advisors recommended, and as long as we all maintain a humble heart desiring only His will, I doubt if we ever will.

Submissive Children

You may be wondering what all this has to do with raising children. I am finally getting to that. In this book I have suggested several channels by which God releases His grace into the lives of your children.

- **A godly heritage:** Before they are even born, or as soon as you understand the truth yourself, you will want to break the power of generational sins and curses that is pouring negative energy into your life and the lives of your children. You will want to establish a channel of pure blessing that floods your home with grace.

- **Saving grace:** As soon as they are old enough to understand, you will want to lead them into a saving knowledge of Jesus Christ, ensuring that they are truly born again.

- **The voice of God:** You will then immediately want to begin encouraging them to respond to the voice of the Holy Spirit Who now lives within them, Who will guide, direct, and sanctify them. As they grow physically, you will respect their growth spiritually as well, encouraging them to turn to the Spirit of Truth in them for wisdom in every aspect of their lives.

- **Decision making:** You will allow them to make decisions from the time they are very young, and as they grow and their decisions become more significant, you will help them learn to hear from God so that their every thought may be full of the wisdom that is from above.

- **The Fifth Commandment:** You will honor your own father and mother, setting an example before your children of godly respect and esteem. You will have faith in the promise of God that as you do so, He will cause your life to be blessed.

- **The Golden Rule:** You will practice the Golden Rule in your home, in your relationships with your spouse and your children. You will treat your children the way you want them to treat you, each other, and all men. You will do for your children whatever you would want them to do for you, being an example that they may follow as you follow Christ.

- **Mutual respect:** You will respect your children as children of God whom He has placed in your care for a short period of time. You will recognize that they were made in the image of God, and, when they have been born again, they are partakers of the divine nature. They are co-heirs with you of the grace of God and they are your brothers and sisters in Christ.

- **Your words:** You will be careful to speak only words that will bring grace to your children. You will never speak words of insult or mockery to your child. You will never deliberately embarrass, humiliate or demean your child, publicly or privately. Your nicknames will express love and respect for them. You will encourage them with the truth of who they are in Christ and that through Him, they can do anything.

- **Their gifts of grace:** You will focus your attention on their strengths, and your energy on increasing their gifts. You will not magnify their weaknesses and failings in any area – socially, academically, athletically or spiritually. You will yourself learn daily how to more completely draw on the grace of God to make you all He has planned for you to be, and you will train your children how to do the same.

- **Your gifts of grace**: You will prayerfully seek the Lord's will for you and your children concerning homeschooling, work and ministry, and you will draw on His grace to do as He desires.

- Essentially, you will be your children's mentor in Christ, discipling them as they grow in the Lord, just as you would any other newborn believer. They will learn to submit to you as you demonstrate your submission to your counselors and as you seek the Lord together with them. You will never offer your children your own limited, human wisdom, but will always listen to the Spirit before offering them any counsel.

Year upon year you will rejoice in watching your children grow in wisdom and stature and in favor with God and man. They will grow in grace and in the personal, intimate knowledge of their Lord and Savior Jesus Christ. And the day will come when you will release them into His keeping, recognizing that they are now adults who must continue on their journey without your vigilant oversight.

How Old Is Old Enough?

But at what age do we consider our children "grown up"? When are they adults who can and must hear from God for themselves and be responsible before God for their own decisions? I have known Christians who raised their children with the expectation that when they turned 18, they were on their own. They would be required to either move out or begin paying rent if they wanted to continue living with their parents. I have also known Christians who go to the other extreme, expecting their children to remain in their home, and in an essentially "child" position, dependent and obedient, until they marry. What is the right answer?

The Bible doesn't give a clear, specific solution to this dilemma. Therefore, we must all seek the Lord for wisdom in our own situation. That is what I want to encourage you to do. Seek the Lord with journaling. Ask Him specifically how

He wants your children raised and when He sees them as accountable to Him.

With some trepidation, I will share with you how He has led us. I recognize that it may seem to be a somewhat radical position to some of you, but that's okay. We're used to being considered crazy. I am not saying that our answer is right for everyone. In fact, it emphatically is not. It is only a feasible response to children who have accepted Jesus as their Lord and Savior, who have demonstrated their ability to recognize the Spirit's voice within their own hearts, and who are daily walking in submission and obedience to the Spirit and the Word of God. Children in any other category must be dealt with differently, as the Spirit leads you.

We dedicated our children to the Lord, and ourselves as parents, as soon as we learned we were expecting. We accepted the Lord's call of stewardship over these two special creations of His, knowing that they were never wholly ours but that they were only entrusted to our care. Our confidence was in Him, that He would use us to raise and train them to be all that He has destined them to be.

Charity and Joshua accepted the Lord and were baptized in the Holy Spirit when they were very young. Mark can still remember the day when Charity was eight years old that he taught her how to recognize the voice of the Lord within her. They were in our swimming pool relaxing, just the two of them. Mark told her how to quiet her own thoughts, look into the spirit world to see Jesus, then notice the spontaneous thoughts that popped into her mind in response to a question she had asked. Right there in the pool, she heard from the Lord for the first time, and later that day she wrote down her conversation. She has been journaling ever since. Joshua also learned to recognize the Spirit's voice within him and has been walking in that relationship from an early age.

We also taught the kids about how God can speak to us through our dreams at night, and Charity, especially, has become skilled in the art of dream interpretation. She recognizes many times when the Lord has emphasized to her heart in a dream something that He had told her in journaling but which she was reluctant to act upon.

We have encouraged Chari and Josh to hear from the Lord

for themselves since they have been able to. We have taught them to come to us for confirmation and correction, and demonstrated that they can trust us to give answers not based on our human inclinations and wisdom but from the Word and the Spirit of God. They have demonstrated that they feel free to talk to us about anything, without fear of judgment or recrimination or ridicule.

The Age of Accountability?

While the Bible itself does not define the age at which children become responsible in God's eyes, Jewish culture and tradition can perhaps give us a clue. Under Jewish, Talmudic Law, boys become obligated to observe the commandments at age 13, girls at age 12. This is known as *Bar Mitzvah*, which literally means "son of the commandment." (A girl is *"Bat Mitzvah"* or "daughter of the commandment.") This happens automatically at the appropriate age; no ceremony is needed to confer these rights and obligations. A 13-year-old boy is automatically a *bar mitzvah*, whether he performs the ceremony and celebrates with a party or not. The ceremony is simply a formal marking of the individual's assumption of the obligation to observe the commandments, along with the corresponding right to take part in leading religious services, to count in a *minyan* (quorum), to form binding contracts, to testify before religious courts, and to marry.

The *bar* and *bat mitzvah* are not the goal of a Jewish education, nor are they a graduation ceremony marking the end of person's Jewish education. Jews are required to study the Scriptures throughout their lives, and some rabbis actually require a *bar mitzvah* student to sign an agreement promising to continue his Jewish education after the *bar mitzvah*.

"The age for *bar mitzvah* is not an outdated notion based on the needs of an agricultural society, as some suggest. This criticism comes from a misunderstanding of the significance of the *bar mitzvah*. *Bar mitzvah* is not about being a full adult in every sense of the word, ready to marry, go out on your own, earn a living and raise children. The *Talmud* makes this abundantly clear ... *Bar mitzvah is simply the age when a person is held responsible for his actions* and minimally qualified to marry."[1]

While we, of course, are not under Jewish Law, especially Talmudic Law, the principles of the *bar* and *bat mitzvah* are consistent with the Lord's leading in our lives. We have expected our children to hear directly from the Lord for themselves and be directly responsible to Him since their early teens. As said earlier, this was not a surprise that was sprung upon them at that age. Like the young Jewish *bar mitzvah* students, Charity and Joshua had been in training for several years. They had been taught how to recognize the voice of the Holy Spirit within them. They had been trained and mentored in the use of the Leader's Paradigm for making wise decisions. They had been practicing their decision-making skills. And they had developed an attitude of submission. They were therefore prepared to take their place as son and daughter of grace.

'Tweens, Teens, and Twenties

There are many decisions that must be made in the life of the 11- to 21-year-old believer. These years can be a great time of training in wisdom, if we will deliberately use them in this way. There are decisions that a child must make every day:

"What will I eat?"
Examining the information available about the effects of various foods upon the body's weight and health can be a valuable exercise for you and your children. Considering the near epidemic teenage problems of obesity on the one extreme and the eating disorders of anorexia and bulimia on the other, the decisions about one's diet should not be considered unimportant. A healthy lifestyle is essential to the overcoming individual who will fulfill his destiny.

After you have researched thoroughly together, each of you should then individually ask the Lord for His will for your diet. Use journaling, and ask expecting Him to answer. Then come together again to share what you have each received. Be open to the possibility that some members of your family may be called to a higher standard than others, based on the plans the Lord has for them in the future. Receive what each one believes he has heard from God with an open heart, listening to the Spirit for His confirmation or adjustment. Do not respond out of your own personal thoughts or prejudices. If you want your children to be submissive to you, they must be able to trust you to be the oracles of God to them, saying only what He wants to say.

"What shall I wear?"

Particularly in the teenage cultures, the way one dresses is extremely significant. One's clothing identifies him or her with a particular belief system and lifestyle – Gothic, grunge, gang, preppy, jock or nerd, to name but a few. The provocative style that many teen girls adopt sends a message about their morals that they may be completely unaware of, and which may actually be misleading. The insecurity of the teen years can lead your Christian teen to dress in order to fit in with a certain group or to appear to be other than he is in his heart.

In the Sermon on the Mount, Jesus said that He is interested in the clothes you wear, so you can go to Him in faith for direction and instruction in this important issue. Dialogue with your children about all the different styles of dress they are aware of and what each represents to them. Without sounding preachy or judgmental, let them know how adults view the various fashions popular with teens. Let them share with you how teens view the various "uniforms" adults choose. Discuss the image each of you wants to project of yourselves, and why that image is important to you. Talk about ways you can each dress to enhance that image.

Then, individually seek the will of the Lord concerning how He wants you personally to dress. At this point, don't ask Him questions about anyone but yourself. Be open to the possibility that He may want you to do some changing, too! Later, come together with your kids again to share what you have each received from the Lord. Listen to the Holy Spirit with your inner ears while listening to each other with your physical ears. If they believe they have heard the Lord say something that you doubt was really the Lord, gently and respectfully ask if they are repeating the Lord's words exactly, or if they are paraphrasing what they think He said. Sometimes we read our own meanings into the Lord's words that make us think He said something He really didn't.

If they are reading exactly what they believe they heard and you believe the Holy Spirit is waving a caution flag at you, express your concerns and suggest that each of you go back to the Lord for more dialogue about the issue. Make sure that your own heart and motives are pure, and that you are only seeking the will of the Lord in the matter. Don't let your own ideas and prejudices get in the way of the pure flow of God's voice to you.

If, when you come together to share again what you have each heard from the Lord, you are still unable to come to consensus, review together again the principles of praying with an idol in your heart (on pages 43–45 of *Communion with God*) and testing your journaling (Chapter 15 of *Communion with God*). Keep in mind that *you* might be wrong, not your child. (Highly unlikely, I know, but possible!) If you both have hearts that are wholly submitted to the Lord and His will, the Holy Spirit Who lives within each of you will give you the wisdom needed to come to peace together.

"With whom shall I spend my time?"
Friends, like clothes, are often an integral part of the teen's personal identity. God is very concerned about who we all choose as friends, peers and models.

> *"Do not be deceived: 'Bad company corrupts good morals.'"*
> (1 Corinthians 15:33)

> *"He who walks with wise men will be wise,*
> *But the companion of fools will suffer harm."*
> (Proverbs 13:20)

On the other hand, Jesus Himself was criticized by the religious legalists of His day for spending time with the pub owners and sinners and prostitutes. If we are to be like Jesus, reaching out to heal the spiritually sick, how can we stay away from those foolish people who would corrupt our good morals?

We each must hear the direction of the Lord clearly to make wise decisions on this issue. It is so easy to let our emotions get in the way of the still, small voice of God. Our children can be blinded by their loyalty to their "undesirable" friends, while we can be as equally blinded by our fears for their safety and spiritual walk. Keep the lines of communication between you and your children open, especially in this important area. Process your fears in the presence of the Lord so you can speak to your children with a pure heart. Encourage (not browbeat) them to journal about their friends. Pray for and expect the Holy Spirit Who lives within them to lead them to truth.

I was privileged to be present at a conversation between mother and daughter at a pastor's home we were visiting in England. Mark was to be speaking at their church that evening at a specially arranged seminar. The daughter, Julie, was about 18 years old and was just finishing one level of school. Her friends were gathering at a local pub for a last party together before they all went their separate ways. Julie was trying to decide where she should go: the church or the pub. (A pub is not just a bar in England; it is actually a casual restaurant. It is not unusual for a Christian to have a meal at a local pub.)

It was clear that she and her mother had a very close and honest relationship with each other, for she was able to discuss her dilemma without fear of judgment. I know many preachers' wives in a similar situation would have said that there was no decision to be made. They had a guest speaker at their church who was actually staying in their home, and of course Julie would come to church.

However, this mother had greater wisdom and greater faith in the Holy Spirit to work in the life of her child. She very calmly listened to Julie's dilemma and all of her reasons for wanting to be at each place. Then she asked her questions, not in a challenging or accusing manner but as someone just making conversation. Who all would be at the party? Were they her close friends? Would she have opportunities to see them again before they went to university? What would it be like at the pub? (Loud and smoky, Julie decided.) Would that be the best place to make her goodbyes? Did she have any responsibilities at the church? Was anyone depending on her for anything? Was she interested in what Mark would be sharing? Would she have the opportunity to hear it again?

In the end, Julie decided to attend the seminar and participated on the worship team. She made the decision herself, but because she had the right kind of relationship with her, her mother was able to influence her without resorting to laws and decrees. And, in the process, Julie was mentored in the art of wise decision-making.

Who? What? Where? When?

As you can see, the 'tween, teen, and twenties are an ideal time to guide your children into the habits that will prepare them for leadership in whatever discipline God calls them to. Some of the most far-reaching decisions of their lives are made during this crucial time. What will they study? Where will they work? Who will they marry, and when? Where will they live? What will their vocation be?

Unfortunately, many people enter adulthood without having ever thought about how they do make decisions, or how they should. Without a clearly thought-out paradigm to guide them, they may depend on their emotions one day, peer pressure another, cold logic another, and the will of God another. One of the greatest gifts we can give our children to prepare them for life is a thoughtful, workable system they can rely upon to help them make wise, godly decisions.

"Go ye!"

By the time Charity was thirteen years old, she had been hearing from God through journaling for five years. Therefore, when she came to us saying that she felt called to go on a short-term mission trip with Teen Mania Ministries, we took her seriously. I had some fears and hesitations, but I realized that they were manifestations of my flesh, not sensations of the Spirit. Mark and I both were convinced in our spirits that Charity had heard from God on this, so we encouraged her in

every way possible, even though my mother's heart quaked at
the thought of my little girl going off to a foreign country
with strangers. It was a time of growing in faith for both
Charity and me, and none of us have ever questioned that it
was truly God's direction in her life.

For the next three years, Chari received the leading of the
Lord to participate in more short-term missions trips. When
she was sixteen, the Lord led her to embark on a one-year
internship at Teen Mania headquarters, which at that time
was in Tulsa, Oklahoma. It was very, very difficult for me to let
her go, but I had confidence in her ability to hear from God
and nothing the Holy Spirit was saying to me indicated that
she was mistaken. It was a wonderful year for her spiritually,
and there is no doubt it was the Lord's will for her at that
time.

I was grateful that the Lord led her back home after her
internship, where she continued her education and short-
term missions experiences. Then, one spring, as she was
looking through the brochures of various mission organiza-
tions, she realized that the Lord was not quickening any of
the opportunities to her spirit. As she prayed about it, she
realized that the Lord did not want her to go anywhere that
year. We confirmed her understanding of the Lord's will for
her to remain at home to focus on completing her degrees
and work with us in our ministry. For her, this was as great a
sacrifice as going to the mission field would be for other
young people. She has a heart for those who have never heard
the Gospel and thrives on the challenges of the missionary
experience.

For five years, she looked longingly at the brochures that
arrived each year detailing all of the available opportunities.
Yet she was obedient to the peace of God in her heart to
devote herself to preparing for the next phase of her life rather
than following the desires of her soul. Finally, when she was
23 years old, the Lord once again released her to short-term
missions. She was led to undertake a prayer-walking tour of an
Islamic country, which was a new form of evangelistic work
for her. God had been pouring into her His Word and His
character and His heart, and now He was ready to send her
forth once more.

Arrows in His Hand

> *"Behold, children are a gift of the LORD;*
> *The fruit of the womb is a reward.*
> *Like arrows in the hand of a warrior,*
> *So are the children of one's youth.*
> *How blessed is the man whose quiver is full of them."*
>
> (Psalm 127:3–5)

God has given us children as His gift and reward, but He has given them to us for a purpose. An arrow is not intended to remain in the hand of a warrior. An arrow is made to be released. It does not achieve its destiny until the warrior takes aim and lets it go!

> *"The LORD called Me from the womb;*
> *From the body of My mother He named Me.*
> *He has made My mouth like a sharp sword,*
> *In the shadow of His hand He has concealed Me;*
> *And He has also made Me a select arrow,*
> **He has hidden Me in His quiver.**
> *He said to Me, 'You are My Servant . . .*
> *In Whom I will show My glory.'"* (Isaiah 49:1–3)

Our children have been called by God from before the foundations of the world. He has known them and called them by name from the time He formed them in the womb. He has preserved and protected them by His own hand. And He uses us parents, fallible and imperfect though we are, to shape our children into select arrows for His use. Our children are not merely "in our quiver," but they are also in the Lord's. He wants to show His glory through them as they are released into the destinies for which they were created.

What Do You Say, Lord?

It's time for you to listen to the Lord again. Ask Him to show you how tightly you are holding on to your children. Ask Him how He wants you to raise them, and at what age He wants you to release them into the responsibility of hearing from

Him for themselves. Ask Him how you can train them so they are ready for this awesome responsibility, and to overcome your own fears about letting them go.

Are you prepared to seek the Lord with your children? Are you a submitted person? Does your life demonstrate that submissive spirit before your children? Are you able to hear the pure words that God speaks about your children, or do your fears, prejudices, and traditions prevent you from hearing clearly? Are you willing to allow the Lord to purify your heart so that His grace may flow more freely to you and through you to your family?

What specific assignment does the Lord have for you right now? What has He said to you through this book that is a high priority? How does He want you to go about implementing the principles?

Don't take anything from this book and try to accomplish it with your own wisdom and in your own strength. Develop a lifestyle of constant communion with God. Lean not on your own understanding, but trust in Him to direct your ways. Seek Him, listen to Him, obey Him. He is the only Source of the grace you need to make your home a heaven on earth and prepare your children as choice arrows in His hand, destined to bring glory to His Name.

Note
1. *Judaism 101: Bar Mitzvah, Bat Mitzvah and Confirmation.* C5756–5761 (1996–2001), Tracey R. Rich, Webmaster@JewFAQ.org, emphasis added.

Appendix A

Leader's Paradigm

The Leader's Paradigm
on pages 160–161 is
© 1995 Christian Leadership University
(716) 652-6990
Permission grranted to reproduce
for teaching purposes

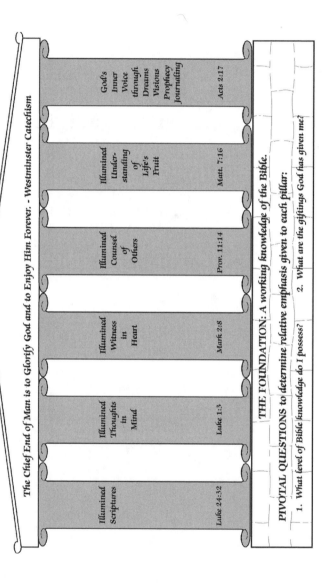

THE LEADER'S PARADIGM

- For creative decision making
- Built upon the skillful interaction of the six pillars
- For discovering truth

The Chief End of Man is to Glorify God and to Enjoy Him Forever. - Westminster Catechism

Illumined Scriptures	Illumined Thoughts in Mind	Illumined Witness in Heart	Illumined Counsel of Others	Illumined Understanding of Life's Fruit	God's Inner Voice through Dreams Visions Prophecy Journaling
Luke 24:32	Luke 1:3	Mark 2:8	Prov. 11:14	Matt. 7:16	Acts 2:17

THE FOUNDATION: A working knowledge of the Bible.

PIVOTAL QUESTIONS to determine relative emphasis given to each pillar:

1. What level of Bible knowledge do I possess?
2. What are the giftings God has given me?

The Leader's Paradigm for Discovering Truth

Pillar number	Key verse	How experienced...	How compared...
Pillar 1 – Illumined Scriptures (Luke 24:32)	*And they said one to another, Did not our heart burn within us, while he talked with us by the way, and while he opened to us the scriptures?* (KJV).	This pillar is experienced as the Holy Spirit illumines Scriptures to us – we sense them leaping off the page or just coming to our attention spontaneously	This pillar could be viewed as enhanced Biblicism. We go beyond studying the Bible with our intellects only, asking for the Holy Spirit to illumine Scriptures to our hearts and minds.
Pillar 2 – Illumined thoughts in one's mind (Luke 1:3)	*It seemed fitting for me as well, having investigated everything carefully from the beginning, to write it out for you in consecutive order, most excellent Theophilus.*	This pillar is experienced as the Holy Spirit guiding our reasoning process through spontaneous impressions. It is obvious that Luke's gospel was more than simply investigative research of his own mind, as what he wrote has stood as the Word of God for 2000 years.	This pillar could be viewed as enhanced rationalism. We go beyond simple rationalism to allowing the Holy Spirit to guide our thinking process (through combining intuition and reason) rather than guiding it ourselves.
Pillar 3 – Illumined witness in one's heart (Mark 2:8)	*And immediately when Jesus perceived in his spirit that they so reasoned within themselves, he said unto them, Why reason ye these things in your hearts?* (KJV).	This pillar is experienced as an impression perceived in your spirit. Deep inner peace or unrest is often part of this experience.	This pillar could be viewed as enhanced hedonism in that one is doing what "feels" good: however, in our case, we are going with the "feel" within our hearts, rather than the "feelings" of the flesh.
Pillar 4 – Illumined counsel of others (Proverbs 11:14)	*Where no counsel is, the people fall: but in the multitude of counselors there is safety* (KJV).	This pillar is experienced as one asks his/her spiritual advisors to seek God for confirmation, additions, or adjustments in the guidance he senses God has given him.	This pillar could be viewed as enhanced humanism, as we are receiving counsel through others; however, we go beyond people's wisdom and ask them to impart the wisdom of God to us.
Pillar 5 – Illumined understanding of life's experiences (Matthew 7:16)	*Ye shall know them by their fruits. Do men gather grapes of thorns, or figs of thistles?* (KJV).	This pillar is experienced as one asks God to give him insight and understanding concerning the fruit life is demonstrating. God gives him revelation as to what has caused the fruit.	This pillar could be viewed as enhanced empiricism, in that we are examining life carefully; however, we go beyond our own limited understanding of life and ask God to give us His understanding of what we are seeing.
Pillar 6 – Illumined revelation from God through dreams, visions, prophecy, and journaling (Acts 2:17)	*And it shall come to pass in the last days, saith God, I will pour out of my Spirit upon all flesh; and your sons and daughters shall prophesy, and your young men shall see visions, and your old men shall dream dreams* (KJV).	This pillar is experienced as you receive direct revelation from God through dreams, visions, and journaling. Journaling is the writing out of your prayers and God's answers.	This pillar could be viewed as enhanced mysticism; however, we go beyond just "any" spirit-encounter as we pursue Holy Spirit-encounter.

THE OBJECTIVE: To have all six pillars in agreement before making a major decision.

Appendix B

Four Keys to Hearing God's Voice

The age in which we live is so married to rationalism and cognitive, analytical thought that we almost mock when we hear of one actually claiming to be able to hear the voice of God. However, we do not scoff, for several reasons. First, men and women throughout the Bible heard God's voice. Also, there are some highly effective and reputable men and women of God alive today who demonstrate that they hear God's voice. Finally, there is a deep hunger within us all to commune with God, and hear Him speak within our hearts.

As a born-again, Bible-believing Christian, I struggled unsuccessfully for years to hear God's voice. I prayed, fasted, studied my Bible and listened for a voice within, all to no avail. *There was no inner voice that I could hear!* Then God set me aside for a year to study, read, and experiment in the area of learning to hear His voice. During that time, the Lord taught me *four keys that opened the door to two-way prayer.* I have discovered that not only do they work for me, but they have worked for many thousands of believers who have been taught to use them, bringing tremendous intimacy to their Christian experience and transforming their very way of living. This will happen to you also as you seek God, utilizing the following four keys. They are all found in Habakkuk 2:1, 2. I encourage you to read this passage before going on.

▶ *Key 1 – God's voice in our hearts sounds like a flow of spontaneous thoughts. Therefore, when I tune to God, I tune to spontaneity.*

The Bible says, *"The LORD answered me and said . . . "* (Habakkuk 2:2). Habakkuk knew the sound of God's voice. Elijah described it as a still, small voice (1 Kings 19:12). I had always listened for an inner *audible* voice, and surely God can and does speak that way at times. However, I have found that for most of us, most of the time, *God's inner voice comes to us as spontaneous thoughts, visions, feelings, or impressions.* For example, haven't each of us had the experience of driving down the road and having *a thought come to us* to pray for a certain person? We generally acknowledge this to be the voice of God calling us to pray for that individual. My question to you is, "What did God's voice sound like as you drove in your car? Was it an inner, audible voice, or was it a spontaneous thought that lit upon your mind?" Most of you would say that God's voice came to you as a spontaneous thought.

So I thought to myself, "Maybe when I listen for God's voice, I should be listening for a flow of spontaneous thoughts. Maybe spirit-level communication is received as spontaneous thoughts, impressions, feelings, and visions." Through experimentation and feedback from thousands of others, I am now convinced that this is so.

The Bible confirms this in many ways. The definition of *paga*, the Hebrew word for intercession, is "a chance encounter or an accidental intersecting." When God lays people on our hearts for intercession, He does it through *paga*, a chance-encounter thought, accidentally intersecting our thought processes. Therefore, when I tune to God, I tune to chance-encounter thoughts or spontaneous thoughts. When I am poised quietly before God in prayer, I have found that the flow of spontaneous thoughts that comes is quite definitely from God.

▶   *Key 2 – I must learn to still my own thoughts and emotions, so that I can sense God's flow of thoughts and emotions within me.*

Habakkuk said, "I will stand on my guard post and station myself on the rampart ... " (Habakkuk 2:1). Habakkuk knew that in order to hear God's quiet, inner, spontaneous thoughts, he had to first go to a quiet place and still his own thoughts and emotions. Psalm 46:10 encourages us to be still, and know that He is God. There is a deep inner knowing (spontaneous flow) in our spirits that each of us can experience when we quiet our flesh and our minds.

I have found several simple ways to quiet myself so that I can more readily pick up God's spontaneous flow. Loving God through a quiet worship song is a most effective means for me (note 2 Kings 3:15). It is as I become still (thoughts, will, and emotions) and am poised before God that the divine flow is realized. Therefore, after I worship quietly and then become still, I open myself for that spontaneous flow. If thoughts come to me of things I have forgotten to do, I write them down and then dismiss them. If thoughts of guilt or unworthiness come to my mind, I repent thoroughly, receive the washing of the blood of the Lamb, and put on His robe of righteousness, seeing myself spotless before the presence of God (Isaiah 61:10; Colossians 1:22).

As I fix my gaze upon Jesus (Hebrews 12:2), becoming quiet in His presence, and sharing with Him what is on my heart, I find that two-way dialogue begins to flow. Spontaneous thoughts flow from the throne of God to me, and I find that I am actually conversing with the King of kings.

It is very important that you become still and properly focused if you are going to receive the pure word of God. If you are not still, you will simply be receiving your own thoughts. If you are not properly focused on Jesus, you will receive an impure flow, because the intuitive flow comes out of that upon which you have fixed your eyes. Therefore, if you fix your eyes upon Jesus, the intuitive flow comes from Jesus. If you fix your gaze upon some desire of your heart, the intuitive flow comes out of that desire of your heart. To have a pure flow you must first of all become still, and secondly, you must carefully fix your eyes upon Jesus. Again I will say, quietly worshiping the King, and then receiving out of the stillness that follows quite easily accomplish this.

▶ *Key 3 – As I pray, I fix the eyes of my heart upon Jesus,*
seeing in the spirit the dreams and visions of Almighty
God.

We have already alluded to this principle in the previous paragraphs; however, we need to develop it a bit further. Habakkuk said, "I will keep watch to see," and God said,

"Record the vision" (Habakkuk 2:1, 2). It is very interesting that Habakkuk was going to actually start looking for vision as he prayed. He was going to open the eyes of his heart, and look into the spirit world to see what God wanted to show him. This is an intriguing idea.

I had never thought of opening the eyes of my heart and looking for vision. However, the more I thought of it, the more I realized this was exactly what God intends for me to do. He gave me eyes in my heart. They are to be used to see in the spirit world the vision and movement of Almighty God. I believe there is an active spirit world functioning all around me. This world is full of angels, demons, the Holy Spirit, the omnipresent God, and His omnipresent Son, Jesus. There is no reason for me not to see it, other than my rational culture, which tells me not to believe it is even there and provides no instruction on how to become open to seeing this spirit world.

The most obvious prerequisite to seeing is that we need to look. Daniel was seeing a vision in his mind and he said, "I was looking ... I kept looking ... I kept looking" (Daniel 7:2, 9, 13). Now as I pray, I look for Jesus present with me, and I watch Him as He speaks to me, doing and saying the things that are on His heart. Many Christians will find that if they will only look, they will see. Jesus is Emmanuel, God with us (Matthew 1:23). It is as simple as that. You will see a spontaneous inner vision in a manner similar to receiving spontaneous inner thoughts. You can see Christ present with you in a comfortable setting, because *Christ is present with you* in a comfortable setting. Actually, you will probably discover that inner vision comes so easily you will have a tendency to reject it, thinking that it is just you. (Doubt is Satan's most effective weapon against the Church.) However, if you will persist in recording these visions, your doubt will soon be overcome by faith as you recognize that the content of them could only be birthed in Almighty God.

God continually revealed Himself to His covenant people using dream and vision. He did so from Genesis to Revelation and said that, since the Holy Spirit was poured out in Acts 2, we should expect to receive a continuing flow of dreams and visions (Acts 2:1–4, 17). Jesus, our perfect Example, demonstrated this ability of living out of ongoing contact with Almighty God. He said that He did nothing on His own initiative, but only that which *He saw the Father doing, and heard the Father saying* (John 5:19, 20, 30). What an incredible way to live!

Is it actually possible for us to live out of the divine initiative as Jesus did? A major purpose of Jesus' death and resurrection was that the veil be torn from top to bottom, giving us access into the immediate presence of God, and we are commanded to draw near (Luke 23:45; Hebrews 10:19–22). Therefore, even though what I am describing seems a bit unusual to a rational 21st Century culture, it is demonstrated and described as being a central biblical teaching and experience. It is time to restore to the Church all that belongs to the Church.

Because of their intensely rational nature and existence in an overly-rational culture, some will need more assistance and understanding of these truths before they can move into them. They will find this help in the book *Communion with God* by the same authors.

► **Key 4 – Journaling, the writing out of our prayers and God's answers, provides a great new freedom in hearing God's voice.**

God told Habakkuk to record the vision and inscribe it on tablets ... (Habakkuk 2:2). It had never crossed my mind to write my prayers and God's answers as Habakkuk did at God's command. If you begin to search Scripture for this idea, you will find hundreds of chapters demonstrating it (Psalms, many of the prophets, Revelation). Why then hadn't I ever thought of it?

I called the process "journaling," and I began experimenting with it. I discovered it to be a fabulous facilitator to clearly discerning God's inner, spontaneous flow, because as I journaled *I was able to write in faith for long periods of time*, simply believing it was God. I did not have to test it as I was receiving it (which jams one's receiver), because I knew that when the flow was over I could go back and test and *examine it carefully*, making sure that it lined up with Scripture.

You will be amazed when you attempt journaling. Doubt

may hinder you at first, but throw it off, reminding yourself that it is a biblical concept, and that God is present, speaking to His children. Don't take yourself too seriously. When you do, you become tense and get in the way of the Holy Spirit's movement. It is when we cease our labors and enter His rest that God is free to flow (Hebrews 4:10). Therefore, put a smile on your face, sit back comfortably, get out your pen and paper, and turn your attention toward God in praise and worship, seeking His face. As you write your question to God and become still, fixing your gaze on Jesus, who is present with you, you will suddenly have a very good thought in response to your question. Don't doubt it, simply write it down. Later, as you read your journaling, you, too, will be blessed to discover that you are indeed dialoguing with God.

Some final notes
No one should attempt this without having first read through at least the New Testament (preferably, the entire Bible), nor should one attempt this unless he is submitted to solid, spiritual leadership. All major directional moves that come through journaling should be submitted before being acted upon.

Appendix C

Suggestions for Groups

We encourage the leaders of every group exploring *Rivers of Grace* to use the books listed in the Bibliography to deepen their understanding of the various subjects discussed and their skill in ministering the grace of God in each area. Be prepared to share further insights from your meditation on the recommended books and to answer questions others might bring to your gathering. You will often be specifically encouraged to lead the group in journaling exercises and into inner healing. Our books *Communion with God* and *Prayers That Heal the Heart,* and the related cassettes, will teach you how to do these if you are unsure.

Following are recommended questions to explore together. These are merely a jumping off place; be sensitive to the leading of the Holy Spirit and the specific needs of the members of your group.

You will notice that each chapter will include questions about the application of previous chapters. These are not here just to give you more to talk about. This book is calling the reader to break old habits and develop new ones. This is not an easy task. By reinforcing the previous chapters' teaching and regularly discussing how it is being applied, you will be providing the accountability and support most of us need to establish lasting change in our lives. Just learning about the ways God's grace can come into our children's lives will be useless if we do not apply what we learn. This regular reinforcement may be the most important purpose of exploring this book in a group.

Chapter 1 – Start with a Clean Slate

The river of a godly heritage is unique in several ways. First, it is a pure gift from your heavenly Father and your human ancestors. This river is already flowing (or already clogged up) before you are even born. While the areas we will look at in future chapters may require diligent effort on your part to change long-established behaviors, this channel can be cleared immediately by your prayer of faith.

1. If the idea of generational sins and curses is new to you, or if you are left with unanswered questions after reading this chapter, take the time to explore it further. This is too important for you to miss out on because of incomplete understanding or a lack of faith. Meditate on the Scriptures given throughout the chapter. Prayerfully read the books recommended in the Bibliography. If you still have questions, write them down and bring them to your group meeting.

2. Are there "besetting sins" that seem to appear in successive generations of your family? Do addiction, temper, infidelity, violence, pride, cynicism, deception, or other sinful attitudes or actions have a hold on several members of your extended family? Is there an area of weakness in your own life that you see in one of your parents, an area you have repeatedly brought before the Lord in repentance and sorrow, only to fall again and again? Is there evidence of generational sins at work in your home and family? "Confess your faults one to another, and pray for one another, that you may be healed" (James 5:16).

3. Are there any hereditary diseases that plague your family? Is there a tendency to be "accident-prone"? Do diligent work and faithful service fail to receive their deserved rewards? Do generation after generation of children who were raised in the Lord waste long years wallowing in the pigsty of the world before eventually returning to their roots? Do others consistently get the credit and rewards for the work your family members do? Is there strong resistance to the Gospel throughout generational lines?

Are there other evidences of curses at work in your home
and family?

4. Are you the blessed recipient of a godly heritage? Can you
   see how the grace of God has been flowing in your home
   and family because of the faithfulness of your parents
   and ancestors?

5. Do you believe that Jesus Christ has broken the power of
   every curse through His death on the cross? Do you
   believe that you can be freed today from every generational sin and curse that may be coming down upon your
   head?

6. Do you recognize the importance of seeing with the eye
   of faith what the Holy Spirit is accomplishing in the spirit
   world? Do you know the power of vision to increase and
   release faith? Do you accept the importance of applying
   the grace of God directly at the point of need? Do you
   understand that, since the power of generational sins and
   curses became activated in your life when you were but a
   baby in your mother's womb, it is necessary to *see* the
   grace of God at work breaking that power over that baby?

7. When everyone in the group has received a clear picture
   from the Holy Spirit of the generational sins and curses at
   work in their own family trees, and is comfortable with
   using the power of vision to focus their faith, you are
   ready to pray together.

   (**Leaders**: Guide the group in the prayer recommended
   by Derek Prince, found at the end of Chapter One. Say a
   sentence, then have the group echo you. Give time for
   the Holy Spirit to bring to mind specific sins that need to
   be renounced and specific individuals who must be
   forgiven, at the appropriate times.

   Then ask the Holy Spirit to give each one a picture of
   him/herself as a tiny baby in his or her mother's womb.
   Ask that each may see the cross of Jesus Christ being
   placed between that baby and all the negative forces of
   previous generations' sins and curses that are trying to
   steal, kill and destroy the joy, health and life of the baby.
   Continue leading the group in the rest of the prayer
   recommended by Mark Virkler. Allow a moment of

silent meditation when you finish, so the Spirit has a chance to complete His work in each heart.)

8. Spend some time in praise to the Lord for setting you free from the power of the past and for establishing a new, godly heritage for all future generations.

9. Over the coming weeks, the Holy Spirit may make you aware of areas of sin in your own life that are providing the enemy with legal grounds to keep you under a curse. Proverbs 26:2 declares that *"a curse without cause does not alight."* As soon as the Spirit makes you aware of any cause within you that allows a curse to attach itself to you, renounce it, thoroughly repent and turn away from it, breaking its power over you by the authority of the cross of Jesus Christ. If you are sensitive to the Spirit as He continues to cleanse you, you will eventually be completely free of the power of your past.

10. Be aware that sins you commit in the future may pollute this river of grace, and unconfessed sin will even begin to dam it up again. As soon as the Holy Spirit convicts you of any sin, be quick to repent and renounce it, breaking its power and preventing the enemy from using it against you and your children.

Chapter 2 – What Is Your Goal?

1. Is the idea of having a clear-cut goal toward which your parenting efforts are focused new to you? Do you think it is a realistic concept? Does it contradict any of your other beliefs, like free will?

2. Did you recognize any of the sample families (the Blushers, Braggins, Brokins, Beemees, or Betterways)? Were you raised in one of these families? What effect has it had on your life? Have you been able to forgive your parents for their mistakes and sins against you?

    (**Leaders**: Be prepared for a time of ministry if the Spirit is working in people's hearts. You may want to lead an individual or the whole group into a prayer of forgiveness of their parents and repentance for their anger and bitterness toward them. Inner healing may also be necessary, if there are deep wounds.)

Do you find yourself treating your children the way you were treated, even though you swore you would never do such a thing? Do you see yourself in any of the other imaginary parents? Why are you like that? Ask the Holy Spirit to show you what is wounded or sinful in your own heart that leads you to act this way. Allow Him to purify your heart so that the only thing that influences the way you parent is the way God parents you.

3. Have you and your spouse talked about what you want to accomplish as parents? Have you discussed the criteria you will use to determine your successfulness as parents? Have you talked about what methods of discipline you will use? Have you thought about the relationship between your goals and your disciplinary philosophy?

4. What specific attitudes, character traits, and skills do you want to see in your children at age five? Age 10? Age 15? Age 21? Age 50? What are you doing to make it happen?

5. The authors indicate that the ability to make wise decisions was a high priority for them. Is this something that you had thought about before reading this chapter? What do you think about the ways the authors went about training their children in decision-making? Are there other ways you can think of to train in wisdom? What have you done or what do you plan to do to train your children in this skill?

6. How old do you believe one must be to be born again? How old were you? Do you know anyone who was born again at a very early age (five or four or even three years old)? Was their salvation genuine? Have your children been born again? If not, what are you doing to encourage the salvation of your children?

7. Do you believe that everyone who is born again has or should have the ability to hear the voice of God within his own heart? Are you able to recognize the Lord's voice in your heart? Do you have daily conversations with Him? Do you think the average Christian needs to hear

from God personally on a daily basis, or is the revelation of the Bible all we need today? How comfortable are you saying, "The Lord told me ..."? How important do you think it is to identify the voice of the Spirit to you? If you are not confident about your ability to distinguish the Lord's voice in your own heart, do you wish you were? If so, what are you going to do about it?

8. Do you believe that children who are born again have or should have the ability to hear the voice of God in their own hearts? What place does the voice of God have in sanctification? What is the relationship between sanctification and Christian parenting? What is the relationship between the voice of God (or intimacy with God) and the law (or rules and regulations)?

   The authors state that their overriding goal in parenting is to have children who recognize and are obedient to the voice of the Holy Spirit within their hearts. Is this a goal that you have embraced in the past, or are interested in embracing now? Why or why not? What effect would this have on your parenting? What effect would this have on your philosophy of discipline? What is the relationship between the voice of God in the believer's heart and the power of grace in his life? Is raising your children in grace rather than law something you might be interested in doing? If so, what foundations must you lay? What steps is the Holy Spirit calling you to take right now?

9. Study Appendix B – Four Keys to Hearing God's Voice. These keys, when used together, have proven highly effective in training Christians of all ages from all over the world how to recognize the voice of the Spirit within their own hearts.

   (*Leaders*: Guide the group in a journaling exercise, *using all four keys*. [Refer to the tapes by Mark Virkler if you need help with this.] Suggested questions you may want to ask the Lord include: "Lord, how often do You want to talk to me?" "Lord, what is the place of law and grace in raising my Christian children?" "Lord, how can I help my children know Your voice within them?"

"Lord, how can I better release Your grace into my family through the river of Your voice?" "Lord, is there anything in my life that is allowing a curse to remain attached to me and my family?" Share with one another what the Spirit has said to you, that you may encourage and support each other. If the Lord gives you specific instructions, purpose in your spirit to be obedient, and draw upon His grace to do so.)

10. If you need to improve your ability to discern the Lord's voice in your heart, don't waste any time seeking out help in doing so. Purchase the books recommended in the Bibliography and devote yourself to growing in this area. Make your commitment known to your group, that they may encourage you and hold you accountable. The Lover of your soul is waiting and longing for you to come to Him.

11. If you are not sure if your children are able to identify the voice of the Spirit within them, find out how the Lord wants you to train them in this vital skill and begin this week.

12. Have you noticed any effects in your life or your family's lives since you broke the power of generational sins and curses? Has the Spirit made you aware of any habits, attitudes or sins in your life that were giving the enemy legal right to leave any curse attached to you? Did you repent and renounce it? Did you break the negative power over you? Are there habits that the Spirit is calling you to break? Share with your friends that they may stand with you in the coming weeks.

Chapter 3 – Honor Your Father and Mother

1. Do you agree that the commandment to honor our parents was given to adults as well as children? What does it mean to honor our parents when we are five years old? 15 years old? 21 years old? 40 years old?

2. Did the Holy Spirit convict you of any sinful attitudes toward your parents? Have you repented? Does He want you to apologize to them for anything? (He doesn't

always, but if He does, be obedient!) Did your parents treat you so badly that you cannot forgive or honor them, at least in your own strength? Are you willing for the Lord to heal your heart and give you His grace to do so, if not for their sake or even for God's sake, then for your own sake and the sake of your children?

(*Leaders*: Be prepared to minister inner healing to anyone who needs it. If you are unfamiliar with this ministry, refer to the books recommended in the Bibliography.)

3. Are there ways in which the Lord is calling you to express greater honor toward your parents (or their memory)?

   (*Leaders*: Guide the group in a journaling exercise, using all four keys, in which they specifically ask, "Lord, are You happy with my attitude and behavior toward my parents? Is there any way in which You want me to change so that I am honoring them the way You want me to?" Share with one another what the Lord says, that you may encourage and support each another in your growth.)

4. In the past week, has the Spirit made you aware of any habits, attitudes or sins in your life that were giving the enemy legal right to leave any curse attached to you? Did you repent and renounce it? Did you break the negative power over you? Are there habits that the Spirit is calling you to break? Share with your friends that they may stand with you in the coming weeks.

5. Have you been able to recognize the Lord's voice more accurately and more often in the past week? Have you been spending more time in daily communion with Him? Has this had any effect on your personal life of faith?

6. Did you do anything this week to encourage your children in their relationship with God? Are your children born again? Have you talked with them about their salvation experience? Have you talked with them about the Holy Spirit Who now lives within them? Do they know that He wants to guide them through their daily lives? Are they able to recognize His voice?

7. Think about the goals for your children that you identified in Chapter Two. What did you do this past week that
   moved you all in the direction of achieving these goals?
   Did you run into any difficulties? Did you change your
   mind about anything? Did you see any positive signs of
   progress?

8. Have you been able to decrease your emphasis on laws
   and rules in your home, and increase your faith in the
   grace of God to guide your children into good decisions
   and behavior? What have you done this week to help
   your children learn to make better decisions?

Chapter 4 – The Golden Rule

1. Discuss situations in which you would act differently if
   you applied the Golden Rule than if you applied the
   Silver Rule. In what ways does the Golden Rule reflect the
   character of Christ more than the Silver Rule does?

2. Have you actively been applying the Golden Rule to your
   closest (family) relationships? Why or why not? What
   effects would it have on your relationships if you were
   more consistent in applying the Golden Rule?

3. Is there a relationship between the Golden Rule and the
   Law of the Harvest (or the Law of Sowing and Reaping)?
   The Law of Increase is a corollary to the Law of the
   Harvest. How does this apply to the Golden Rule and its
   effect on your family?

4. Think back to the behaviors and character traits you want
   to see developed in your child (Chapter 2). How can you
   utilize the Golden Rule to encourage the growth of these
   qualities? What specifically can you do to your children
   that you want them to do to you and others? Share with
   the group the list of priorities that God gave you for your
   children, and your part in treating your children the way
   you want them to treat you and others (exercise found at
   the end of Chapter 4).

   (*Leaders*: If the majority of the group has not already
   done this exercise, or did it only as an exercise of the
   mind, use this question for a group journaling exercise.)

5. In what ways has your personal view of God been influenced by the way you were treated by your parents? Because they were loving and giving, is that how you see God? Because they were critical and stingy, is that how you expect God to be? Is your ability to believe the promises of God more influenced by the character of your parents than by the Word of God? Do you need to forgive your parents for shaping your expectations this way? Do you need to repent for not recognizing that God is greater than your parents?

   (*Leaders*: Be prepared to lead the group in a prayer of forgiveness and repentance, if the Spirit so leads. Inner healing may be necessary if deep wounds are revealed that are strongly affecting one's ability to trust God.)

6. In what ways were you able to show honor to your parents in the past week? Were you obedient to the Lord's voice to you in this area?

7. What did you do this past week toward achieving the goals for your children that you identified in Chapter 2? Did you run into any difficulties? Did you see any positive signs of progress?

8. Are you continuing to have daily communion with God? Share with the group some of the things He has said to you this past week. Are you becoming more confident in your ability to discern His voice in your heart?

9. Are your children increasing in their ability to identify the Lord's voice in their hearts? Do you talk with them about what God is saying to you and what He is saying to them? Are you encouraging them to listen for His voice guiding them in all things?

10. Have you been able to decrease your emphasis on laws and rules in your home, and increase your faith in the grace of God to guide your children into good decisions and behavior? What have you done this week to help your children learn to make better decisions?

11. In the past week, has the Spirit made you aware of any habits, attitudes or sins in your life that were giving the enemy legal right to leave any curse attached to you? Did

you repent and renounce it? Did you break the negative power over you? Are there habits that the Spirit is calling you to break? Share with your friends that they may stand with you in the coming weeks.

Chapter 5 – Respect Everyone in Every Way

1. Do you think it is necessary to show respect to children? Why or why not? Do you subscribe to the belief that "children are to be seen and not heard"? Can you think of occasions when you deliberately embarrassed your child in front of your friends, or his? Do you think this was the behavior of a godly parent?

2. How have you reacted to your child's attempts at self-expression? Are you confident that you were expressing the will of the Lord in your reactions? How do you respond to your child's mistakes, especially (financially) costly ones? How do you want people to react to you when you make a mistake? Is there any reason not to respond this way to your children's slip-ups?

3. What is your child's love language? What are the most meaningful ways to express love to him or her? If you don't know, observe him more closely. Watch how he expresses love. (We often express love in the way it is most meaningful for us to receive it.) When does he "light up"? Ask the Lord specifically, in journaling, how you can best show each of your children your love and His love.

   (**Leaders**: If it is apparent that most of the people in the group have not already done this, do it together as a group, and share what you receive.)

4. What do you think of the Ten-Year Rule? Can you think of a situation in the last month in which applying it would have caused you to make a different decision? Would the new decision have been better in any way? Do you tend to "sweat the small stuff"? Do you want to change? If so, ask the Lord to show you how, and draw upon His grace to do so.

5. Do you ever lie to your children to get them to mind? Do you regularly say no initially, then relent under pressure? Do your children understand that you often say things you don't mean, so nagging is a good way to get their own way? How does God want you to change so that your children will accept your "No" as your final word?

6. Would any of your children be considered "strong-willed"? Have you made every issue, no matter how important, a contest of wills? Is the Holy Spirit asking you to change in any way? How does the Lord want you to respond to their unique gifts?

   (**Leaders**: If most of the group are struggling with this issue, and it is apparent they have not yet made it a matter of journaling, take the time in the group meeting to journal together about it.)

7. In what ways can or should you show respect for your children?

   (**Leaders**: Guide the group into a journaling exercise, using all four keys, in which everyone individually asks God the question: "Lord, how do You want me to show respect for my children? How can I show respect and still maintain my authority?" Share your answers with one another for confirmation, encouragement, and to establish accountability in obeying what He says.)

8. Did you have any opportunities to apply the Golden Rule in your home during the last week? Did you find yourself acting differently than your initial impulse because of your commitment to put it into practice? Are you finding it a struggle to treat your spouse and your children the way you want to be treated?

9. In what ways were you able to show honor to your parents in the past week? Were you obedient to the Lord's voice to you in this area?

10. What did you do this past week toward achieving the goals for your children that you identified in Chapter 2? Did you run into any difficulties? Did you see any positive signs of progress?

11. Are you continuing to have daily communion with God? Share with the group some of the things He has said to you this past week. Are you becoming more confident in your ability to discern His voice in your heart?

12. Are your children increasing in their ability to identify the Lord's voice in their hearts? Do you talk with them about what God is saying to you and what He is saying to them? Are you encouraging them to listen for His voice guiding them in all things?

13. Have you been able to decrease your emphasis on laws and rules in your home, and increase your faith in the grace of God to guide your children into good decisions and behavior?

14. What have you done this week to help your children learn to make better decisions?

Chapter 6 – Watch Your Words!

1. What nicknames were you given by your parents or family members when you were a child? Can you see any way in which they affected you in later years? Have you called upon the power of the cross of Jesus to break the negative influence of those names over you?

2. What pet names do you have for your children when they are good? How about when they are not being so good? How do you describe them to your co-workers? What do you say when you introduce them? Are you speaking curses over them? Are you creating the reality for their future that you want to create?

3. Do you believe there really was power in the father's blessing in Bible times, or was that just a nice tradition, a kind of wrapping up of the father's life before he died? Is there power in a father's words today? If it has changed, why has it? If there is power in a parent's words, what kind of power are you releasing into your children's lives? Is there a blessing the Lord wants you to pronounce over your children?

(*Leaders*: If it is apparent that the majority of the group have not already taken this before the Lord in journaling, do so now as a group.)

4. How can words "give grace to those who hear"? Generally speaking, are your words a channel by which the grace of God can flow freely into your home and children?

5. How often do you tell your children that you love them? Do you clearly say the words, or do you expect them to get the message some other way? Do you demonstrate your love for them in ways that are meaningful to them? Keep track of how often you tell each of your children individually that you love them during the coming week.

6. Do you remember hearing your father say he loved you? How often? Under what circumstances? Are you one of the countless adults who are living under the rejection (real or perceived) of their fathers? Are you willing to receive healing from the Lord for this hurt?

   (*Leaders*: Guide the group into an inner healing exercise in which each one may experience the heavenly Father's love for him or her. You may also want to share insights from *The Father Heart of God* by Floyd McClung and *The Father's Blessing* by John Arnott.)

7. Have you been obedient in expressing respect for your children in the ways the Lord told you to in the past week?

8. Have you been applying the Golden Rule in your home with greater consistency?

9. Have you been obedient to the Lord's voice in showing honor to your parents?

10. Are you continuing to have daily communion with God? Share with the group some of the things He has said to you this past week.

11. Are your children increasing in their ability to identify the Lord's voice in their hearts? Do you talk with them about what God is saying to you and what He is saying to them? Are you encouraging them to listen for His voice guiding them in all things?

12. Have you been able to decrease your emphasis on laws and rules in your home, and increase your faith in the grace of God to guide your children into good decisions and behavior? What have you done this week to help your children learn to make better decisions?

Chapter 7 – Focus on Strengths

1. What subjects were you really good at in school? What subjects did you really enjoy? (Is there a correlation there?) What subjects were a struggle for you? To what extent are you using the subjects in which you did well in your current profession? To what extent are you using subjects that were difficult for you? How happy are you in your current line of work? Are you expressing your gifts? Is your career or occupation a channel of grace for you because it is a place where the gifts of grace God has placed within you are released? If not, I encourage you to journal about alternatives into which the Lord may want to lead you.

2. What are the academic strengths of each of your children? Have you been encouraging them to pursue their areas of interest as fast and as far as they desire? Is there any way in which you could be a greater help and encouragement to them in their quest to become experts in their calling? (This is not to say that every gift and strength is automatically also a calling.) If you have not already done so, ask the Lord through journaling for His guidance in this important aspect of being a good parent.

3. What are the areas of academic weakness for your children? Have you been placing too much emphasis on these areas? Is most of their study time taken up with trying to excel or even become competent in their area of weakness? Are there ways in which you can come alongside to support them in these areas? Are there ways in which you can take the pressure off them in these areas? How much skill or knowledge in this area is absolutely necessary for success in life, to be a good citizen and a thriving Christian? If you have not already done so, ask

the Lord through journaling for His guidance in how to respond to the weakness of your children.

4. What are the character strengths of each of your children? Are there ways in which these strengths are sometimes perceived to be weaknesses? Are there ways in which these strengths need guidance or self-discipline? Are your children aware that you see these strengths in their lives? How can you train your children to recognize the grace of God flowing to and through them through their gifts? If you have not already done so, ask the Lord through journaling for any special instructions He has for raising each of your children individually.

5. What are the character weaknesses of each of your children? In what ways can these weaknesses be used by God and become their strengths? What kind of guidance will your children need in order to learn to submit these weaknesses to God to become channels through which His strength may be perfected?

6. How do you usually approach your own areas of sin and weakness? Do you focus on yourself, your impotence, your sinfulness, your failure, your weakness? Do you struggle to drive out the darkness from your soul by the strength of your will? Can you accept that freedom from sin can be as easy as focusing on the power and purity of Christ within you? Can you look into a mirror and see yourself completely forgiven, pure, spotless and holy, clothed in a white robe of Christ's righteousness? Can you see Christ in you, willing and doing His good pleasure? Can you believe that *He* will complete the work He has begun in you?

   (*Leaders*: Be prepared to present a meditation on Galatians 2:20, the truth of the "Christ I" and the freedom of living naturally supernatural.)

7. How has your communication been this past week? Have you noticed any unwholesome, worthless or corrupt words coming out of your mouth? Have you used only such words as are good for edification according to the need of the moment, so that they give grace to those who hear (Ephesians 4:29)? Have you become more aware of

the nicknames you call your children? How have you been reacting to their mistakes? Did you keep track of how often you told each child individually that you loved him or her? Are you satisfied that it was often enough? Are your children satisfied that it was enough? Is God satisfied? Have your words become a river of God's grace flowing into your home?

8. Have you been obedient in expressing respect for your children in the ways the Lord told you to in the past week?

9. Have you been applying the Golden Rule in your home with greater consistency?

10. Are you continuing to have daily communion with God? Share with the group some of the things He has said to you this past week.

11. Are your children increasing in their ability to identify the Lord's voice in their hearts? Do you talk with them about what God is saying to you and what He is saying to them? Are you encouraging them to listen for His voice guiding them in all things?

12. Have you been able to decrease your emphasis on laws and rules in your home, and increase your faith in the grace of God to guide your children into good decisions and behavior? What have you done this week to help your children learn to make better decisions?

Chapter 8 – Make Them Your Ministry

1. Has your church ever explored the ideas of spiritual parenting or mentoring? Have you ever thought God might want you to mentor a young believer? Have you had any training in doing so? Have you ever considered the possibility that God was calling you to be a mentor to your own children?

2. What do you think about the idea of parenting being a legitimate ministry? Do you agree with the authors that when God gives you children, He calls you to devote yourself to raising them in the Lord, that this is the most important ministry He wants you to fulfill during the

years they are under your care? Do you agree that He may call either parent to dedicate him or herself to this task, or do you believe this is only a calling for men or only for women? What is your scriptural support for your position? Have you or your spouse joyfully set yourself aside to this ministry, as the Lord has led you? What effect has this had on your lives? Are you struggling with it? Have you been criticized by other believer's for your obedience to the Lord in this?

3. What gifts has God given you that can be channels of grace into your family? In what ways does God want your gifts to be a blessing to your family? Have you been offering your gifts within your home, or have you insisted on finding other outlets and beneficiaries of God's grace through you?

4. What are your thoughts on homeschooling? What is the Lord saying to you about homeschooling? Is He calling you into this exciting lifestyle? How are you reacting? Are you angry? Afraid? Frustrated? Excited? Thrilled? If your response is negative, spend time journaling, processing those negative emotions, discovering their root and finding healing and strength in the *rhema* words of God.

5. Have you been obedient to the Lord's word to you about your children's strengths and weaknesses? Have you been focusing more on their strengths this week? How have you been encouraging them to become experts in the area of their calling and giftedness? How have you been handling their areas of weakness? Have you seen any effects in their lives as a result of the changes in your attitude? Have you been able to see Christ in you more clearly?

6. How has your communication been this past week? Have your words become a river of God's grace flowing into your home?

7. Have you been obedient in expressing respect for your children in the ways the Lord told you to in the past week?

8. Have you been applying the Golden Rule in your home with greater consistency?

9. What have you done this past week to show honor to your parents?

10. Are you continuing to have daily communion with God? Share with the group some of the things He has said to you this past week.

11. Are your children increasing in their ability to identify the Lord's voice in their hearts? Do you talk with them about what God is saying to you and what He is saying to them? Are you encouraging them to listen for His voice guiding them in all things?

12. Have you been able to decrease your emphasis on laws and rules in your home, and increase your faith in the grace of God to guide your children into good decisions and behavior? What have you done this week to help your children learn to make better decisions?

Chapter 9 – Release Them in Faith!

1. Were you at all affected by the "Discipleship Movement" of the 1960s and 1970s? Have your experiences left scars that influence your beliefs about submission today? Is your theology a product of your wounds or the revelation of the Word of God by the Spirit of God? Do you need healing because of abuses of authority you have suffered, either through the Discipleship Movement or within your local church?

   (**Leaders**: Be prepared to minister inner healing and forgiveness if the Spirit leads in this direction.)

2. What is your current understanding of authority and submission? To what extent are we "under" other people who know God's will for us better than we do? To what extent are we "alone" as we stand before God to answer for our actions? Are there lines of authority in the kingdom, and if so, what are they? Who is to be submitted to whom? What if you disagree with those "over you in the Lord"? What are you supposed to do if you believe God

told you one thing and your authority tells you something different?

3. At what age does the Holy Spirit begin speaking in the heart of a believing child? At what age can a child learn to recognize and be obedient to the voice of the Spirit within him or her? At what age is a child responsible before God for his obedience to His Spirit? What effect does that have on parenting a believing child?

4. What does it mean to release your children in faith? At what age does God want you to release your children? Is it a specific age, or when a specific milestone is passed (e.g., when they marry)? How are you all preparing for this day?

5. Which of the chapters of this book has been most challenging for you? Are you struggling with the truth of the teaching, or with the implementation of that truth in your family life? If you are struggling with the application of the teaching, remember that it is Christ Who will do the work, if you will call upon Him in your moment of need.

6. Which of the chapters of the book has been the greatest blessing to you? In what ways have you been able to change your attitudes and behaviors so that the rivers of God's grace may flow more freely into your home and family? What results have you already seen?

7. What are you going to do to be sure you do not lapse back into old habits and clog up those rivers once again?

   (**Leaders**: Guide the group in a journaling exercise, asking the Lord for wisdom in how to continue along the path you have begun. Share with one another what the Lord says, that you may encourage and support one another.)

Bibliography

Chapter 1 – Start with a Clean Slate
Prayers That Heal the Heart by Mark and Patti Virkler
Blessing or Curse: You Can Choose by Derek Prince
Free Masonry – Invisible Cult in Our Midst by Jack Harris

Chapter 2 – What Is Your Goal?
Leading Little Ones to God by M. Schoolland
Living with Jesus: Welcome to God's Family by Daphne Kirk
(a workbook to do with your young children to lead them
to Christ)
Living with Jesus: Talking and Listening by Daphne Kirk
(teaching your young child to journal)
Learning to Communicate with God by Kay Velker and Mark
Virkler (teaching your young teens to journal)
Communion with God Study Guide by Mark and Patti Virkler
(teaching older teens and adults to journal – workbook
format)
Dialogue with God by Mark and Patti Virkler (same
teaching as *Communion with God* but in a more narrative
format)
"The Leader's Paradigm for Decision-Making" is included in
Communion with God Study Guide and in Appendix A of
this book

Chapter 3 – Honor Your Father and Mother

Counseled by God by Mark and Patti Virkler (contains a
chapter on inner healing)

Prayers That Heal the Heart by Mark and Patti Virkler
(contains teaching on inner healing)

Emotionally Free by Rita Bennett (on inner healing)

Chapter 5 – Respect Everyone in Every Way

Language of Love by Gary Smalley

Chapter 6 – Watch Your Words!

The Blessing by Gary Smalley

The Gift of the Blessing by Gary Smalley

Blessing or Curse: You Can Choose by Derek Prince

The Father Heart of God by Floyd McClung

The Father's Blessing by John Arnott

Chapter 7 – Focus on Strengths

Naturally Supernatural by Mark and Patti Virkler

The Great Mystery by Mark and Patti Virkler

God Unlimited by Norman Grubb

Chapter 8 – Make Them Your Ministry

The Christian Home School by Greg Harris

If you have enjoyed this book and would like to help us to send a copy of it and many other titles to needy pastors in the **Third World**, please write for further information or send your gift to:

Sovereign World Trust
PO Box 777, Tonbridge
Kent TN11 0ZS
United Kingdom

or to the '**Sovereign World**' distributor in your country.

Visit our website at **www.sovereign-world.org**
for a full range of Sovereign World books.